The Marriage Encounter

The Marriage Encounter

·AS I HAVE LOVED YOU·

FR. CHUCK GALLAGHER, S.J.

DOUBLEDAY & COMPANY, INC.
GARDEN CITY, NEW YORK
1975

Library of Congress Cataloging in Publication Data

Gallagher, Chuck, 1927–
The marriage encounter.

1. Marriage counseling. 2. Group relations training. I. Title.
HQ10.G336   362.8′2
ISBN 0-385-00991-7
Library of Congress Catalog Card Number 75–12224
Copyright © 1975 by Marriage Encounter, Inc.
All Rights Reserved
Printed in the United States of America
First Edition

ACKNOWLEDGMENTS

This whole book could be a series of acknowledgments because so many people have made it possible, most particularly, those who came to the raps in Ireland, Belgium, Canada, Australia and all over the United States, and who were so open and honest and generous in their sharings. Charlie and Lee Rooney and Father Ed Hauf helped me so much in the initial stages of this manuscript. Pam and Fritz Schaeffer were absolutely tireless in going over the book, line by line, and Charlie and Annette Buondelmonte who proofed this book so lovingly. Their generosity is overwhelming. Mary and Phil Coffey did so much legwork for me. My faithful secretary, Janette Sobey lived under the pressure of having a boss who is a "last-minute Johnny" about deadlines. My executive couples have spent themselves beyond measure: Ed and Harriet Garzero, Jim and Maddie Harper and Bob and Geri Campbell.

With awe and warm, tender love toward the dialoguing couples and priests of Marriage Encounter; they have made me who I am.

Contents

Foreword

After five years of being deeply immersed in the Marriage Encounter movement, an editor from Doubleday called on an otherwise beautiful day and asked, "How about a book on Marriage Encounter?" My first reaction was, "My own words are coming back to haunt me." I had always said I would do anything for the couples and priests in Marriage Encounter. Now I was being put to the test. Quite honestly, I was the most reluctant dragon you'd ever want to see. I'd much rather give a Marriage Encounter weekend than try to describe it, even less write about it. Furthermore, anybody who knows me realizes it's much easier to get me off my backside than to get me on it. So my first reaction was a flat-out William Tecumseh Sherman type of response—"No way." However, editors are persistent souls and about a year later he came back again. This time the answer was a foot-dragging "Yes." The motivation behind my change of heart was the need our couples and priests have to share their experience with relatives and friends. This book is not really intended to stand on its own. No book can actually explain Marriage Encounter. Hopefully, it will fill out the knowledge of someone who has a Marriage Encounter couple or priest as a member of the family or as a friend. Marriage Encounter is not a thing, it's people. Marriage Encounter is more easily experienced than defined.

Even with my "yes" there were still some reservations, serious and compelling ones. Would those who read the book use it to bypass the experience of the weekend? Would some try to practice the technique of dialogue on their own without the atmosphere of the weekend or the experience of the team couples and priests? Would the entire Marriage Encounter movement be judged on the basis of this book? Would the various reactions to the book affect those who were already Encountered? These and so many other questions went through my mind. Another very present fear was that people who had difficult marriage situations would flock to our weekends instead of seeking out the professional advice and direction they need. So I sat down with the people of Marriage Encounter and shared these worries with them. These concerns were also theirs. However, it just seemed we had grown to such proportions that not to speak ourselves to the broader general public would be like an elephant tiptoeing through a house. Furthermore, all sorts of magazine articles have been written and even some books, so we decided to go ahead and trust in you, the reader.

There are two requests we make of you, with great sincerity and much earnestness. Please, please do not try to substitute this book for the weekend. Nothing can replace the weekend; it must be experienced. There is no way you can practice the Marriage Encounter dialogue technique without having made a weekend. The second equally strong request is to recognize that Marriage Encounter is for good marriages; it is not a therapy or a counseling program. It is for couples who have basically good communication with each other but want more.

We do not believe that Marriage Encounter is the only good thing available today. The Church is rich with the presence of the Spirit. Jesus promised to be with us until the end of time. The diversity and variety of deep goodness in the Church today holds out joy and hope and love to all. One movement can at best express a tiny fraction of the wealth and beauty of the Church, and its tender concern for people . There are so many wonderful manifestations of the Spirit in today's Church: Charismatic Renewal, Directed Retreats, Liturgical Renewal, Focolare, Cursillo, to name a few. The list is endless. Marriage Encounter is one of the expressions of the vitality and love present in the Church.

Marriage Encounter is beautiful—not more beautiful than the others or less so—simply gorgeous in itself.

I have experienced the life of Marriage Encounter, practically since its beginning in this country. I have formed deep roots into the community of couples and priests who have made Marriage Encounter and have continued the experience in their daily lives. I have been, and continue to be, privileged to be a familiar of their minds and hearts. So I'm not trying to describe Marriage Encounter as an event or as a thing, but to share with you, the reader, the experience of people I am identified with and who call me their own. In a very real way, it is not my book, it is our book. This book was prepared by sitting down with close to a thousand couples and priests in the United States, Ireland, Belgium and England. Many of the couples and priests I had never met before, and yet we were all family—linked together by the experience of the Marriage Encounter weekend and the practice of daily dialogue. We would meet in someone's living room and I'd throw out general questions such as: "What was the most significant thing that happened to you on your Marriage Encounter weekend? What was your reaction when you were asked to write on the weekend? What effect did making the weekend have on your marriage? What does the concentration on feelings mean to you? What does daily dialogue mean to you and would you ever give it up?" Then I just wrote down whatever they said. What was so magnificent was the uniqueness of each individual and yet, at the same time, the commonality of their experience. The couples I met with set the tone and atmosphere of this book, even though only a small percentage of them have been quoted here. They are some of the happiest, freest people I've ever known, with the best marriages I've ever seen and they probably are among the best with which the world has been graced.

So this book is not a history of Marriage Encounter, nor does it give the full character of the movement. It's merely an introduction for readers who are unfamiliar with the outline of the weekend and the dialogue technique, or for those who want to know more. Basically, as I mentioned above, what I'd like this book to be is one that Marriage Encounter people could give to relatives and friends. I'm certainly not trying to speak for everyone, but just for a representative sampling of Marriage Encounter couples and priests. My concentration is mainly on the weekend and the dialogue afterward. Another whole book could be written on various key concepts in Marriage Encounter.

There is another reason peeking out from my heart. I love couples and I don't know anything that has such a big immediate impact with such long-term results as Marriage Encounter. So I have a yearning in my heart for every couple in this whole wide world to make a Marriage Encounter.

Preface

As I experience the extraordinary happenings in today's wonderful Church, I have become intrigued by the operating procedures of the Holy Spirit. It has been customary to recognize His presence in the fruitfulness of endeavors where He is at work. But lately I have noticed another of His telltale signs, the *unexpected* way He goes about renewing the face of the earth.

As a bishop, I have sensed His presence in the *unexpected* good things He seems to have going in the Church, without so much as prior notice to our chancery offices! I saw Him in the *unexpected* directions of Vatican II and the *unexpected* jolly genius of John XXIII. Now I recognize Him in the *unexpected* new and peaceful developments emerging from post-Vatican II ecclesiastical jitters.

I see Him in the *unexpected* new interest of the laity in the Spirit's top priority, holiness; in the faithful's new, warm, encouraging support of their beleaguered clergy; in the simple enthusiastic rediscovery of the early Christians' love in Christ, prayerfulness, Bible reading, family life, and penance.

Among God's people in whom the Spirit seems to be moving so *unexpectedly* are the lovable lovers of Marriage Encounter.

Marriage Encounter is an extremely practical experience which teaches a sound technique of loving communication between spouses. The dialogue taught on the weekend, and used on a regular basis thereafter, gives couples a brief time each day to work on their marriage relationship.

Husbands and wives become freshly aware of how precious

they are to each other. It is like a second honeymoon as they discover anew that their relationship is in Christ, that it mirrors Christ's relationship to the Church. After the weekend, they sense a yearning to share their newly enriched love with others.

On my own Marriage Encounter weekend, and in sharing with couples and priests throughout the country, I have experienced the marvelous contribution of Marriage Encounter to a growing loving relationship of couples and priests within the Church. The weekend made me warmly conscious that a bishop or priest in love with his people shares a beautiful gift with husbands and wives who are in love with each other: namely, the model of Christ in love with His Church.

Couples who have made the Marriage Encounter learn that the Church is lovingly concerned about their marriage relationship. Encounter helps couples to grow out of a humdrum existence, to polish the sterling silver of their marriage, and to make it radiant as Our Father intended.

The weekend puts job, children, finances, and friends in proper perspective so that couples no longer seem to take each other for granted. The Marriage Encounter weekend and follow-up program are designed to make good marriages better and better marriages great.

Daily dialogue is designed to renew basic human communications between spouses in such a way as to promote a fresh sacramental way of life that is in, through, and for the Church. Dialogue helps couples strive toward that loving unity which is God's plan for them (". . . and the two shall be one") by enabling husbands and wives to express themselves to one another honestly, lovingly, and nonjudgmentally.

In a way, daily dialogue, as proposed by the Encounter community, renews daily the celebration of the Sacrament of Matrimony. The spouses, in sharing their real selves briefly each day, decide to recommit themselves to one another. They say "I do" again and again. It is an ongoing, daily striving to be one. It is the daily decision to love each other more and more.

Experiencing the effort to meet the real needs of our people and observing how the laity in the best Vatican II spirit are rallying to the aid of each other and the broader Church community, I give thanks for this sign of the Spirit moving *unexpectedly* in the Church. Christian marriages were great "in the good old days," and they give promise now of being even greater "in the good new days."

Devotedly yours in Christ,
MOST REVEREND EDWARD A. MCCARTHY
Bishop of Phoenix

The Marriage Encounter

Introduction

"All that is necessary for the triumph of evil, is for good people to do nothing," said Edmund Burke. The Christophers have pointed out time and time again that "it is far better to light one candle than to curse the darkness." Every election day we are reminded our vote does make a difference. One of the ancient Greeks was convinced if he could only find a place to stand for leverage, he would be able to move the world.

All my life long, these statements and similar ones have been made to me by my Mom and Dad, teachers, confessors, friends. As a senior in high school I remember very vividly the story that a priest, of whom I thought the world, told about World War II. As the story goes, some American soldiers had fought all day for a small town in Germany. Then, just before nightfall, they captured it. When they marched into the village square, there lying in pieces was a statue of Christ which had been knocked off its pedestal by the artillery bombardment. Over the course of the next several days, they gathered it all up and carefully began to put it together. On finally completing the job, they discovered the hands were missing. Nonetheless, they decided to put it back on its pedestal. The next morning a crudely lettered cardboard sign was hanging across the handless arms. It said, "I have no hands but yours."

It was an inspiring moment for me. I had a very vivid picture of Jesus standing in the midst of His people yearning to touch them, to wipe away their tears, to encourage with a pat on the back, to console with an embrace. He seemed to be looking at me and telling me He needed me. I have carried that image with me through the years. It gave me a sense of worth, of value, of importance. Furthermore, it gave me hope for my world and what I could do for it. I didn't want to go through life just living. I wanted to accomplish something. Avoiding evil wasn't enough. I wanted to live in a world that was loving and good, the way it was supposed to be.

I believed this with all my heart, but it got harder and harder to see where I was having any real effect. Oh yes, I stayed up late hours to counsel parents and it helped them. Many went away from my confessional healed and encouraged. Kids came on retreat and saw a new dimension to their lives. But it seemed to stop there. Oh, of course, those in immediate contact with the ones I touched were affected, but it didn't go beyond that.

So many good people I knew who were concerned and caring broke their backs reaching out to people with the same results. It was good and meaningful for the people with whom they were in direct contact but it stayed there.

Our world had remained essentially the same, despite the example of people like the Christophers. Even with the thousands of candles that had been lit, the darkness of this world was still with us. War was endless. After countless sit-ins and Supreme Court decisions, "black is beautiful" was still a "whistling past the graveyard" statement. Two thirds of the world still lived in poverty and exploitation; drugs seemed prevalent; the number of divorces was catching up to the number of marriages; violence was becoming part of the air we breathe; the Church was fighting old and irrelevant battles.

No, Edmund Burke, we the good people, are not "doing nothing." So how come evil is still triumphing? Good just doesn't seem to spread the way evil does. It helps those directly involved, but it just doesn't reach out there and have an impact on that great world. The temptation was not for all of us to stop trying, but to stop hoping. We were like a football team behind by twenty points in the closing moments of a game. We weren't going to

quit; we were still going to do our best, but the realities were
very stark. We could get high marks on our individual perform-
ances in the game, but the results were going against us. It was a
strong temptation to stop looking beyond our immediate horizons and settle down into doing what we could, but not expecting too much.

Then a handful of years ago on a dingy off-Broadway stage,
Richard Kiley was singing a song which was to become one of
the most popular songs in the world, "The Impossible Dream." It
reached into the secret places of people, touched our hearts and
gave voice to our hidden and most precious hopes and dreams. It
had a great melody, but what really turned us on was that we
found part of ourselves in that song. It spoke us. All of us have a
heavenly cause, an unreachable star we long to reach. We know
we have the resources to fight the unbeatable foe.

Just about the same time, Marriage Encounter appeared here
—definitely an off-off-Broadway production. It went on in retreat
houses and businessmen's motels, bungalow colonies and old
novitiates. Now seven years later it is becoming one of the most
popular experiences in the world. As this book is being written,
over 200,000 couples in the United States alone have made a
Marriage Encounter, plus thousands across the world, from Canada to India, Australia to Belgium, Ireland to Mexico, England
to Japan. It is growing at the rate of 65,000 couples per year,
though virtually the only method of advertising is word of
mouth, couples who have made the Encounter urging their
friends to go. With no support or promotion outside of itself,
Marriage Encounter has grown from the enthusiasm of couples
and priests who want to share it. The love generated by their
own Encounter experience just spills over; it cannot be contained.

Marriage Encounter is a great experience in itself, but what really gets to the couples who make it is that they find themselves
in it. It speaks who they really are. Love, especially love of one
another, is their "unreachable star," their "heavenly cause," their

"impossible dream." This has been their yearning; now it becomes their "quest."

Their "unbeatable foe" has many faces and uses weapons as subtle as simply taking each other for granted. Their "arms have grown weary" from fighting off routine. They have "marched into the hell" of disillusionment and loneliness, and borne "the unbearable sorrow" of seeing the bright shiny star of hope for their love move further and further away. The "unrightable wrongs" in their lives have been the memories of past hurts.

What is so beautiful about Marriage Encounter is that it is focused on the couple and their love for each other. But when they really listen to one another and are open with and living for their spouse, their horizons broaden to include all of us. They know love isn't love until you give it away, so "the world will be better by far" if they truly, fully and completely love each other.

Marriage Encounter is one of the most widely varied groups of people you can find. There are young, newly married couples and great grandparents, childless couples and parents of large families. There are cops, business executives, nurses, hardhats, Wall Street men, secretaries, farmers, lawyers, truck drivers, teachers, salesmen, repairmen, priests, sisters, brothers, Rabbis, ministers, college professors, grammar school dropouts, regular churchgoers, the religiously indifferent, liberals, conservatives, residents of cities, suburbs and rural areas. The one aspect of their lives shared by all is that they have made a Marriage Encounter weekend, and their common dedication is to seek greatness in their marriage.

Many couples have gone out during the week after their Encounter and bought new wedding rings. They look on their wedding ceremony as the time they began living together; on the Encounter as the time they got married.

Their mutual goal of greatness gives kinship with one another. In Belgium the people are split along language lines the way we are by color. After Encounter, French and Flemish couples who lived beside each other for years without speaking now visit each other's homes and are close friends. In Ireland, the class barriers between blue-collar and white-collar workers is very strong. After the Encounter, they see each other as persons. Cardinal Suenens of Brussels has called the Marriage Encounter one of the three most significant movements within the Church today. Thousands of couples dedicate many of their waking hours to making Marriage Encounter available to everyone. Despite the obstacles and hardships of time away from family and friends, couples have traveled thousands of miles, or just a few, to give weekends and spread the Encounter message; some have made great material sacrifices to make the Encounter available as broadly as possible.

For three years, one couple, as an anniversary present, gave each other a Marriage Encounter. No, they didn't go themselves each time. They gave the money each year to pay the expenses of a whole weekend for thirty couples. Their own weekend meant so much to them that they thought the best gift they could give each other would be to enable others to make the Encounter.

Book jackets are always carefully designed. Highly skilled and imaginative people work long hours to come up with something different, something which will catch your eye and lead you to buy the book. Many hours of conferences are usually spent among designers, editor and author to come up with just the right cover.

For us there never was any doubt. Wherever I went to rap ideas on the book, everyone just instinctively said, "It's got to be our symbol on the cover." The heart, the wedding rings and the cross express love, marriage and the Church—what we are all about. That symbol identifies us to one another and to the world. When Marriage Encounter couples and priests see it in a bookstore window, on a library shelf or on a coffee table, they'll know it is "our" book. It is like the shamrock to the Irish.

That red and gold logo is dear to the hearts of hundreds of thousands of us all over the world. We proudly display a decal on the rear windows of our cars and the front doors of our homes. It is the symbol of our quest to love one another and to give everyone else a chance to do the same. It is the banner we wave as we follow "that star" as we dream the *possible dream.*

That old Greek wasn't so far out after all. There is a spot to stand, and so we can move the world. It's found wherever couples are loving one another.

CHAPTER I

What the World Needs Now . . .

We live in a highly educated society, solid and sensible. People don't jump at the first thing that comes along. Oh yes, there are the shooting-star types, but Marriage Encounter has been going for seven years now and hasn't slowed down yet. Furthermore, there is no big organization, no big money behind it. Marriage Encounter is couples and priests volunteering their newly found enthusiasm in living.

One barrier to trying new things is inertia. Most people live a rather patterned life and it takes something big to get them to move. They would much rather put up with the disadvantages of what they have and are sure of than try something new. So how come there has been such a tremendous response to Marriage Encounter? Why are so many flocking to it? Why does it mean that much to them?

You don't have to be a genius or have a degree in sociology to recognize something is missing today. Headlines scream, professors analyze, politicians bemoan the evident malaise. We don't need them to tell us. We know this. Our hearts are not fully satisfied with the quality of our lives and our personal relationships. Some causes are common knowledge: the break up of neighborhoods and the move to the suburbs; too many people getting married without adequate understanding and preparation; the isolation of the nuclear family; lack of job satisfaction —all of them pointing to the alienation so many feel.

It is one thing to read a magazine article or see a special on TV do a "think piece" on the sociological impact of these various circumstances of today's suburbia. We can agree or disagree with the brilliance of the insight or the correctness of the analysis. The overview helps us to formulate our opinions but it doesn't involve us as persons. When particular applications of these trends pinch in against us, then we tend to respond.

The break up of neighborhoods can be faced intellectually with equanimity, but when we are living in a suburban town where everyone's values are different and no one believes what we believe, when it's our children who are exposed to pot, abortion, indifferent family life—then it's not easy to be objective.

There is a crazy quilt of values, backgrounds and goals of everyone who lives in a suburban town. There is truly nothing to hold them together; there is no basis of unity. As a result people tend to question their own convictions and ambitions and tend to suppress them, lest they be a cause of friction with their neighbors. Common hopes and values in life do more to unite people than any other single factor. When this element is missing, there is no cohesiveness, no sense of belonging to one another.

We are not isolated entities. Human fulfillment and satisfaction in life cannot be defined merely in achievement of individual goals. We want to be important and worthwhile in the eyes of others, most especially those with whom we are in most frequent contact. However, if all those people have diverse aims, we may be important on our terms but not theirs. So we are not involved in their searching in life. We can win respect but not a sense of identity. The opposite of love is not hate—it's indifference. If people shrug off my values—not oppose or get angry at, but merely are unresponsive to them—they don't really love me. They are not being tolerant; they are walking away from me and saying, in essence, that they couldn't care less.

I can look around at the marriage patterns that exist in our society and recognize that too many people are getting married. Some of them are just not prepared—psychologically, mentally or spiritually. But when I'm exposed directly to a couple, as a neighbor or a friend, who falls into one of those categories, then

I'm much more personally upset. I'm not so tolerant about the fact that they're that way and it's a pattern of society. It pinches in on my life. It can be very clear to me in my mind that men and women should be able to have the same opportunity to experience family love even if they're not married. The fact is they're really not offered that chance in the practical order in our society because it's just not an acceptable practice to have an unmarried adult living in our house. I can see that this might be a serious mistake if the single person in question is my own sister. In all probability, her loneliness could lead her to get involved in an unsuitable marriage. It's unsuitable marriages such as these that make the idea of marriage frightening to some people.

There have been many articles written about the dangers of a nuclear family. Most specifically, both husband and wife tend to try to fulfill all their personal and affective needs through one another which creates a tremendous drain. However, it just seems that there is no option in our society, that there is no real support for a more extended form of family life.

Whole books have been written about the "rat race" and what a devastating effect it has on the personal lives of people. Yet, when you're on the treadmill it's very hard to step off it.

The very word "alienation" causes us to wince, because we've been there. We feel buried in a complex and shifting society without a place to put our feet. We often have a purposelessness, a sense of being unimportant, unneeded, unvalued. So we draw in and put our whole attention on just our own little world of family, house and job, but that just doesn't seem to solve the problem. There just has to be more than this.

These are some of the negative forces in our society that make us uncomfortable and have us looking for something that will give us a direction, point out a way, offer a hope for something more.

Marriage Encounter grows and flourishes because couples are willing to face the shallowness of their marriages and family relationships and to seek for a better way to live. Lincoln's statement about fooling people is still true. Good people really aware of their values are starting to assert them. They can be and have been distracted by the multiple and confusing changes our world is experiencing, but their common sense prevails. They recognize that the family is the key to fulfillment and meaning in life. Virtually every couple who gets married wants their relationship to be lifelong and filled with great warmth and closeness. They admire and envy couples who have this kind of relationship. When something like Marriage Encounter comes along that offers a real hope for a deep, enduring and meaningful marriage, people respond. It is difficult to overestimate the importance of this desire for a good marriage. A good marriage is extraordinarily attractive.

Nothing brings out the real personal qualities of a human being such as depth, tenderness, extraordinary generosity and willingness to sacrifice, as does gentle love for another person. We best exhibit interior strength, determination, compassion and dedication to a beloved spouse. Everything in life can come up smelling like roses for a couple, but if they're not in "sync" with one another there is a hollowness in the hearts of both. On the other hand, couples who are really united and close can put up with anything. Marriage Encounter offers a way to build that kind of relationship.

Marriage Encounter doesn't put people in boxes. It doesn't say you have to love in any particular way. Each couple has their own unique love that only they can express. Marriage Encounter, through the dialogue, offers to each couple a way to let the love between them come forth loud and clear, without interference.

Currently, there is much talk about preserving natural resources. We recognize we can be very careless, and have been more prodigal than we realized until we ran into shortages of land, fuel, air and water. Only then did we start looking for alternatives possibly bypassed before as impractical, inconvenient or too expensive. Yet the world's greatest natural resource is love, and the core of human love—the one all other forms of love are founded on and drawn from—is marital love. Ironically, marital love is usually looked upon as very self-contained, nothing the world can use to build a better life for people. It doesn't have to work this way. Marital love can be and should be the gentle power that overcomes isolation and alienation. The obsessive drive for possessions, power and prestige comes from an un-satisfied need deep within all of us to be valued and recognized. Loving couples can give each other this recognition and sense of value so that the need is fulfilled and the grasping drive for things that lead to war, poverty and alienation is absent.

The Church has always been an instrument of God to improve the quality of human life: educating the young; caring for the sick and dying; proclaiming that slavery is against the dignity of human beings; preaching that women are not chattels to be used but persons to be loved and to give love, and that art is an important way for man to express his ideals and dreams. Proba-bly the number one concern of the Church over the centuries has been family values, upholding the tremendous dignity of men and women and the worth of the marital relationship.

Matrimony—the couple—is one of the seven sacraments the Church treasures. Together with sacred Scripture, these are at the heart of what it means to be Catholic. The Catholic Church has accumulated much experience on how to respond to and sup-port couples and offer them the better life. The Church's involve-ment in Marriage Encounter is a very real guarantee to couples that they are not being asked to go off into uncharted seas. Most people are too level-headed and sensible to want to get involved in a fly-by-night program. The truth of the matter is that many people, even nonbelievers, have more faith in the Church than anything else when it comes to marriage. So the priests' partici-pation in Marriage Encounter on a continuing basis (forty have committed their full lives to promotion and progress and another two hundred are heavily involved) gives people a sense of secu-rity, a pledge that it is trustworthy. The presence of the priest reassures good couples who might wonder whether it is a get-rich-quick scheme or a device for social or personal manipulation.

The success of Marriage Encounter depends on the extraordinary fundamental strength of the Catholic Church. The Church provides roots. It is a family. It offers people an identity. It calls beyond ourselves and our selfishness. It calls us to a greatness that is a genuine alternative to what the world offers. It calls couples to love one another deeply and richly beyond temporary attraction and convenience. Marriage Encounter is a living expression of the Church's tender and practical concern for people.

It's been tough being a priest these last ten years or so. So many things dear to me like Mass, Scripture, the Church itself have been undergoing radical change. A lot of good people aren't around any more. It was like seeing your family fighting and then part of it leaving home. So what has been very beautiful for me is the number of people, who once they find each other, find the Church again. It's like a guy taking his best girl home to meet his family. He wants so much for them to see her at her best and to like her the way he does. The Church is my best girl and I want everyone to love her the way I do. It's music to my ears to hear at Encounter meetings the chorus of "I came back."

The dynamite in the couple relationship that gives their love such an explosive impact on those around them is their keen awareness that they are called to live a sacramental way of life. Many couples have returned to the Church and the Sacraments as a result of their Encounter. A constant refrain among Encounter couples is that they had gotten married at the Catholic Church. It was a ceremony. Now they *are marrying* each day in the Catholic Church. Before Catholicism was a practice, now it is an experience. Before it was something they did, now it is who they are. This gives them a sense of mission. A calling to love one another and all people as Jesus has loved them.

The greatest act of faith I was ever privileged to witness was made on a weekend about two years ago. A couple came that was having a great deal of difficulty with their belief in God. The wife wondered whether she believed at all. Both were highly intelligent and educated people who had read a lot of theology and philosophy, but they weren't getting anyplace. Finally, on Sunday afternoon, they dragged themselves to their feet; the words came choking out of their throats: "We don't believe in God but you do, and we want to belong to you, so we make our act of faith." They have more than kept the commitment they made to us.

Fred Weiss looked at the Church both before and after he made his weekend, and said, "Before Marriage Encounter I saw the Church as a dowdy old maid walking down the street about her business with two shopping bags in her hands. If you asked me a couple of minutes after I passed her what she looked like I wouldn't even remember having seen her. Since our weekend I now see the Church as a beautiful woman. I notice every little detail. The color of her eyes, how she wears her hair, the way she walks and talks. I can't keep my eyes off her."

Marriage Encounter is a practical spelling out of Vatican Council II, most particularly the bishop's statement that we, the people, are the Church. Through Marriage Encounter the Church is speaking to the people in a down to earth way, is getting to them in flesh-and-blood terms and people are responding. It is a wonderful experience seeing an idea come to life through the daily lives of couples.

Any daily newspaper is a catalogue of ideas and programs competing for people's attention and involvement. Sensitivity programs, lonely heart clubs, singles' clubs and on and on, everything from the bizarre to the seriously scientific. Some of these things are very popular, others are attractive only to fringe groups, but what their presence indicates is a deep need in people. Many of these programs touch a relatively small number of people and need extensively trained personnel and expensive facilities. By comparison, Marriage Encounter has a wide appeal, makes extensive use of lay people and runs on an austerity budget.

All the above reasons play a part in creating the atmosphere in which couples are receptive to an experience such as Marriage Encounter. The negative aspects in our society nudge couples into looking around for something better, something to compensate for the deficiencies with which they are faced. The positive aspects, most especially their own goodness, give them the ability to respond once they see something worthwhile. They are ready and willing.

I've always wondered whether the early Church ever got used to miracles. Did the stories of Peter and Paul and John's healing ever become commonplace? After a while, did it have to be a "big" one, before people would get excited? Raising from the dead would get the full treatment, but healing a severed finger might be looked on as "another one of those." Could it have been that withered hands didn't rate as high as blindness? Is it possible that news about a boy being cured of a harelip might take second place to gossip about a wedding or the newest hot-shot gladiator in the coliseum? Maybe they even rated the apostles: This one is only good for palsy, this one is a specialist on eyes.

The whole idea seems silly, doesn't it? I started thinking along these lines because I can't for the life of me understand any couple or priest who doesn't rush to make a Marriage Encounter and keep it up through daily dialogue once they have made it. Marriage Encounter is a true miracle. It cures the paralysis of years of taking each other for granted, the palsy of being about all sorts of other things but one another, the blindness of not really knowing the person I'm living with, the deafness of not listening to one another. It raises us not only to new life but to new love.

So when someone tells me that Marriage Encounter is just another one of those movements in the Church, I guess I can believe someone shrugged off Peter's curing a withered hand by saying, "Well, Paul got a leg." When someone says, "We'll get around to Marriage Encounter, maybe," or "What's so special about that?" or "We don't want to go," I guess I can believe people in the early Church, after a while, wanted to be cured by John rather than James, or wouldn't count it if they got sight back in only one eye, or would rather go to the coliseum than talk to Peter.

However, what finally gives them the go-power is the Marriage Encounter couples with whom they are in contact. All the arguments in the world could never persuade anyone to make a Marriage Encounter. An experience is beyond logic. No one can be talked into going; any couple can come up with any number of reasons why they can't or shouldn't or don't need a Marriage Encounter. Couples decide for themselves. What motivates people to want to go on a Marriage Encounter is the living example of those who have gone: the closeness and warmth they observe in Marriage Encounter couples. They don't know what it is, but they see their friends have changed. So they go on a Marriage Encounter and, in turn, their friends are touched. And the beat goes on.

CHAPTER II

The Phenomenon of Marriage Encounter

Before Marriage Encounter I had had a lot of varied experience as a teacher, hospital chaplain, basketball coach, assistant headmaster of a boys' high school, college chaplain, youth retreat master, CFM chaplain. More importantly, I had built friendships with many really good men and women.

Of these, probably my relationship with Brad and Jan Rigdon, presently the executive secretary team of Marriage Encounter, was most typical. In fact, it was to their home I returned the Sunday night of my Encounter weekend shouting, "You've got to go." We'd been friends for some time, but it went beyond personal ties. We were concerned—concerned over what was happening to our world and, above all, to our Church. The three of us saw all sorts of things wrong but we didn't want to be just carpers. We wanted to do something, and we were working hard, but we were really getting nowhere. Nothing the Church said or did seemed to be real to people. Though it was all good and beautiful and true, it didn't hit people where they lived. It all seemed either small potatoes or too idealistic.

Many a night we sat together in their home talking until early morning, planning, hoping, praying. The Church seemed like someone in a foreign land who has a great gift for the people but can't give it, because he doesn't speak the language. Then Marriage Encounter came along with the language of the people, couple love.

One month after I made my Marriage Encounter, Brad and Jan made theirs. We sat in their living room that night, very still this time, afraid almost to say aloud what we were thinking but the joy on our faces telling it all. "This is it! We're on our way. Let's go turn on those couples. They don't know what's in store for them. Yeeeeee-ow!"

I had the same feeling a football player has when he breaks through the line and sees a clear field in front of him. There was freedom and exhilaration. All the pounding away was over and we were going to score. There was no doubt whatsoever in my mind that we were going to touch the hearts of people deeply. Moreover, there would be great joy and richness for everyone involved, and those effects would be felt by the children and then in ever-widening ripples by the whole world. It was a real "Eureka" moment.

It wasn't just us. It seemed to happen to everyone who made a Marriage Encounter. Oona Olsen re-created the evening after an Encounter weekend she and her husband made about three years ago. Around the world thousands of couples echo her words: "Pete and I couldn't sit still after our weekend. We had received so much. We couldn't sleep; we didn't know what to do with ourselves. The weekend showed us the way to what we had wanted in our marriage before we were married, what our marriage had had in the beginning but had somehow lost. The dream was always there; now the vision came back."

Much the same experience was shared by Tom McGuiness: "As I grew up I saw through my parents the possibilities for a life rich and full of love and giving. That is what I really wanted, what I dreamed of. But after a couple years of marriage we got so caught up in the doing: children, job, family and personal responsibilities. It put cobwebs on my dream of love. I remember driving home from that Marriage Encounter weekend in the car and saying, for the first time in my life, I felt free to show the love I had inside of me to Jayne."

Marriage Encounter starts with a weekend about love which provides new perspectives for the couple. In the simplest terms it could be defined as a crash program to learn a technique of communication, and through this communication to experience each other as fully as possible on the weekend. Then the couple can take it home and practice it on a regular basis. It is not a therapy program—Marriage Encounter is for good marriages—nor is it group dynamics. What happens, happens between two married people. It is a unique and beautiful way to discover one another even more deeply than they have up until this time.

Marriage Encounter is not a thing, an event, a happening which occurs outside the couple. It is the couple themselves, experiencing each other through the method of communication that is taught and shared on the weekend. Dick and Cindy Pardi describe its impact: "This method allows people to reveal themselves to each other in a most loving and honest way. It gives them an opportunity to set aside fears and affirm their mutual love in a very tangible, believable way. It gives them an opportunity to receive and accept love. It is through this method that the total Encounter experience happens."

What excited me so in the beginning, and still does, is that a Marriage Encounter holds out a workable plan to make a great marriage a reality. It doesn't ask a couple to quit their jobs, go to the missions or do all sorts of mighty deeds. It merely asks them to do what they had started doing and had wanted to do all along—love one another. It shows them how to get out all the love inside of them.

Marriage Encounter doesn't say to a couple, "We have something you don't have. Let us improve you." No, it really says, "You two are already so beautiful. Come and realize that beauty and continue to discover it in each other your life long."

The basic pattern of the Marriage Encounter weekend is a presentation made by a team composed of a couple and a priest who have deeply experienced Marriage Encounter. There is a series of twelve presentations, each one of which introduces the participating couples to some aspect of the dialogue technique. At the end of each presentation a short period of time is set aside for each individual making the Encounter to engage in personal reflection. This is time just to look inside oneself and discover with greater awareness just who I am, what makes me tick, what is important to me, how does the other person fit into my life. Each couple is made up of two distinct, complete persons. Each of us must be most ourselves in order to be most a couple. At the conclusion of the personal reflection, the couple meets in the privacy of their own room. They exchange with one another what they have discovered about themselves and attempt to reach out to experience each other in depth with love and understanding.

The thematic outline, or sweep of the weekend, goes from "I" to "We" to "We and God" to "We, God and the World." Every we is made up two I's. Furthermore, our relationship with ourselves is the basic underpinning for our relationship with everyone else, including our spouse. It is to the degree that I love myself that I love others. One of the basic problems all of us have, as far as our relationship with other people is concerned, is our lack of reverence and our lack of appreciation of ourselves. This is why we hold back and protect ourselves, because we don't want to get too close to the other person. This is not because we think the other person isn't so good. It's because we don't think we are. The first step of Marriage Encounter is to discover where we stand in relationship with our own selves. To discover what we really think about ourselves, not the way we may appear to others, or the front we put on. But how we feel about ourselves deep down. It is a time of honesty and deep insight.

Then we face "We"—who we truly are to one another. We look at how we started, what expectations were bred into us and looked for in us by other people, what expectations we had of ourselves, where we are in living up to all those expectations, and where we want to be. We look at the two of us and sincerely try to evaluate where we stand with one another. It is a sincere look at our coupleness.

The next phase of Marriage Encounter is to experience how deeply God cares about us and how important it is to Him for us to really enjoy one another as a couple in fully human terms. We become conscious of how much He cares for our well-being in our relationship with one another. It becomes clear that far from being a harsh judge, He is a loving Father. He yearns so much for us to do well with one another. He doesn't want us to do all sorts of right things; He just wants us to love one another.

In We, God and the World, Marriage Encounter brings out the dreams, hopes and ambitions that a couple had when they first met, fell in love, got engaged and were married. They were convinced then that the whole world was enriched by their love for one another. By the end of the weekend that dream is alive again. They have a great tenderness in their hearts for all mankind and for the needs of everyone because of their love for one another. The old saying has it: "All the world loves a lover." That is true because the lover loves the whole world. So by the end of the weekend the couple experiencing it, first and foremost, falls in love with one another all over again in even deeper and richer terms than when they began. Then their love knows no bounds and it includes all of us.

Marriage Encounter starts with the basic premise that marriage is a love affair between two people who are totally and irrevocably committed to one another. It is two people who have chosen to share a lifetime of mutual self-discovery and self-revelation. Their whole purpose as a couple is to celebrate with warmth, tenderness and affection the awesome goodness of their spouse and their rich beauty as a couple. It is a weekend for people who want to become a "we."

"From the very beginning of our marriage," said the Adriaens, "we had a deep urge to get close to one another. Yet, we noticed that even though the desire for closeness was there, separateness had begun to creep into our lives. There was very little oneness in our relationship. So Marriage Encounter really came from heaven as an answer to our search."

The reason a Marriage Encounter must begin with each person looking to see what he or she has to give to their relationship is that in our daily lives we get so bound up with accomplishment, getting ahead or just surviving in this world that we never really spend much time with ourselves. Because we don't, we fail to see our true worth. The experience of Ken Gee is more or less representative. "I had to look very hard at myself," he said, "to see my best qualities. Yet, when I do see them—when I realize my worth as a person—it makes me feel very giving and very loving."

"Before Marriage Encounter, I never seemed to spend much time worrying about finding who I was," Chris Paglia told me. "I rarely considered it possible or even necessary to spend time thinking about myself. If it had occurred to me, I would have had no idea of a direction to take or of guidelines to follow. I'm a doer, and it seemed I should be doing things, not thinking about myself."

Like Chris, few of us take the time for the reflection we so desperately need in our rush-rush, hustle-bustle world. We are a "go, go, go" people under a great deal of pressure to make decisions, solve problems and accomplish things. When we are alone, we often have a television set turned on or a radio playing, a book to pick up or a puzzle to work on, or a phone call to make.

It is important to take time, to step back and look at ourselves, to ask, "Who am I? What does my life mean?" Then, after taking time to reflect, we often find our true selves and recognize our great value. We can say with Len Genovese: "Somehow, somewhere I really became me. I became a whole person instead of half a man." Or with Mary Duphiney: "Stopping to think meant ceasing to be a 'what.' I became softer and more real; I began to experience some of my deeper qualities. My pace became slower, and when my body slowed down, my mind became clearer and more creative."

Because we don't often think about it, we have very little recognition of the full dimensions of our personhood. Very few people use even half of their potential, not because they are deliberately holding back or that they are lazy or distracted, but because they are not even aware of the possibilities. So often lovers say, "You are the only person in the world for me." There is even a song that goes: "I'll Never Find Another You." But the truth is most husbands and wives haven't found each other yet; they've only met each other. The reason for this is that most individuals haven't really discovered themselves in any real fullness, and even what they have discovered of themselves they haven't shared. So an important aspect of the dialogue technique which Marriage Encounter uses is for husband and wife to separate briefly and really get in touch with themselves so that they can then share more deeply with each other. Unless they have a full awareness of who they are as persons, they can't be responsive to any other person, including their spouse. It is sad enough to discover a husband or a wife who says, "I've lived with my spouse for twenty years and we are really strangers." But it is more regrettable when we don't even know ourselves.

One of the questions couples ask when you talk to them about Marriage Encounter is, "Will it hurt?" In a way this question reminds me of a kid sent into a football game. The team is driving down the field, the quarterback is told to call his number. Before going in he looks at the coach and he says, "Will it hurt when I am tackled?" Or like the boy who is falling in love with a girl and he asks his buddy, "Will it hurt if I fall in love with her?" Anybody who heard either the football player or the boy in love asking those questions would be surprised that the question was even on his mind. That really isn't the point in playing football or falling in love. How much can he want to play ball if he is thinking that way? Does he really care about the girl at all? Is he going to score a touchdown only if the tackle doesn't hurt? Are you going to fall in love only if you have a guarantee it can't bring any pain?

On some occasions during the course of a Marriage Encounter weekend, there can be a sense of rejection on the part of the husband, wife or both. After all, we're a little bit out of shape, so we could get some muscle strain from pulling in toward one another. I've kept myself so busy and there are so many things to do, that

I really haven't looked deeply into myself in a long time. What I discover there I may not like to see initially. It could be that, for a while, understanding comes hard in some areas. I may not like to recognize that we have taken each other for granted so many times. So it would be foolish to deny that there can be pain. The alternative of isolation and loneliness, though, holds out even less attraction. The possible hurt on a Marriage Encounter weekend is not the pain of dying, but the pain of coming out of a coma or a birth—it brings new life. Naturally, a husband and wife on the weekend are going to take all steps possible to avoid hurting one another, but not at the risk of avoiding their relationship.

The pain can be real. I know from my own personal encounters on weekends there are so many things about me I'd rather keep to myself. I'd much rather face into me on my own terms than bring someone else into the picture. I want to be strong and very much in control of myself. So there is a ripping when I open up. But the pain is wiped away in the joy of being understood and accepted.

Some couples take each other for granted because they have bought peace at any price. They have avoided the hot pain of confrontation for the cold and numbing ache of isolation. This question of hurt was considered seriously by Vince Stahl. "Being open with my wife sometimes hurts very much," he said. "Not in a physical sense, of course, but in a deeper way. When I'm open I'm most vulnerable to having her see me as who I am right at that moment. Before Encounter I would never admit to having feelings, especially feelings which might bring my masculinity into question—feelings such as fear, loneliness, sadness. I didn't want her to consider me weak and unmanly. But the ability to reveal these feelings has come about by developing confidence and trust in each other. Sharing feelings is an opportunity for us to see each other as we are at that moment."

All the effort and struggle isn't anywhere near the amount of joy that results from this Encounter. "Yes, it hurts!" winces Don Kenny. "However," he said, "it hurt much more in the beginning when I questioned whether or not Chris would accept my openness. I know now that she will—and with all the love I could ever imagine. We've shared tough feelings, and it wasn't easy, but each time our closeness and our love grew. Is it worth it? You bet!" To the question of pain, Father Ed Murray responded, "Of course it hurts, but there was pain without it as well. The difference making it worthwhile is that formerly it was blind pain, stoically endured. Now it is pain enlightened by the vision of Easter. Pain is described by Jesus—the pain endured by a woman in childbirth quickly forgotten once the child is held."

In their sharing, couples find hope. "It was tremendously exciting to me to find we could recover the closeness we had when we were first married and to find that keeping it was within our power," said Duane Elser.

The goal of the dialogue is for couples to revel in one another's personhood the way they did in their days of early marriage. They wanted simply to be together then, to converse with one another. That was more than enough. Their enjoyment in life did not stem from how much money they had, whether they were going to get ahead in this world, how many children they were going to have or their plans for them, or any of the things that occupied their thoughts in later years. It seldom mattered what they did together. What counted was merely being present to each other, and enjoying that presence. Their sentences were sprinkled with *I, you, us.* They were not concerned with things. Their whole world centered around their discovery of one another.

Chris Kenny shared a memory of what it was like in those days: "When Don and I first met, dated and married, we constantly wanted to be together. We were eager to find out as much as we could about each other. Life was exciting, never dull; and we rarely took one another for granted. After ten years of marriage, I began to realize we had somehow lost being Don and Chris and were Don the Daddy and provider and Chris the Mommy and organizer. Don admitted he was comfortable; he didn't want to rock the boat. But I was becoming more unhappy each day, though I couldn't put my finger on the reason. Then came Marriage Encounter and a new way of life."

Marriage Encounter is a work weekend. It is not something done to you or for you. You make a Marriage Encounter. It's the old story of input equals output.

Ray Re found he "went into the weekend with some self-preoccupation and an attitude of superiority that prejudiced me to think of Beth's world as being made up of trivia. This attitude presented a stumbling block to my really listening to Beth. I had to make an extraordinary effort to listen. I would dwell on myself or just drift from Beth, I often had to ask her to repeat herself and I had to concentrate hard in order to focus on her. I didn't think I was doing too well in my effort, but gradually Beth became fuller in my awareness and I became sensitive to her presence and her sincere effort to reveal herself to me."

Marriage Encounter offers "new life" because it is not simply a humanistic experience. More than a communications workshop, beyond the one-dimensional, it is a full experience and therefore deeply religious. As a Catholic experience, it offers a dimension beyond the merely human, while remaining firmly planted in the flesh-and-blood realities of daily living and daily loving. God has a very real stake in how well we love one another. His plan for us to be full of joy with a share in His more abundant life is dependent on our mutual love. Marriage Encounter is a call to each couple to take their Sacrament of Matrimony home with them. The team couples and priest share the deepest experiences of their commitment to each other and of their faith.

Though it is a Catholic experience, the weekend is open to people of all faiths.[1] As each couple is left to experience the weekend in their own way, no one finds the team couples' sharing

---

[1] We have shared the Marriage Encounter experience with the following denominations, which now have their own expressions: Church of Christ, Episcopalian, Jewish, and Reorganized Latter-day Saints.

of their Catholic faith offensive. The fullness of the weekend offers the rich and loving faithfulness of the Catholic faith community but each couple takes as little or as much of it as they wish or translate what is uniquely Catholic into the beliefs of their own church.

Marriage Encounter is for those couples who have a good thing going for them and want to make it better. It doesn't tell people how to be married but offers a means whereby they can discover how wonderful they really are. It is a call to greatness— not as something to be achieved, but as something already there waiting to be recognized. It is the rediscovery of married love.

In a very real way the dialogue technique offers couples an opportunity to discover they have hidden bank accounts all over the place. They realize they are like someone who has millions of dollars and doesn't know it. They have been living on one hundred dollars a week eating franks and beans and drinking beer when they could be having steak and caviar and drinking champagne.

CHAPTER III

The Marriage Encounter Team

Do you think you could ever forget the guy who introduced you to your wife? In a sense, that's what the teams do on a Marriage Encounter. They give you a chance to meet and find one another through the dialogue. They are not experts on marriage. Only you are the expert on your own marriage. They are not professional counselors or theologians. Few couples need that. They are not there to teach you how to be married. Only you can decide that. They are simply everyday garden-variety men and women like yourselves. They are couples and priests who have had a tremendously deep and meaningful Marriage Encounter and were invited to share their experience with others by becoming a team couple or priest. Team couples have discovered how much they mean to each other and are convinced others will make that same discovery for themselves through Marriage Encounter.

Teams care. They care about your love for one another. They have a passion to share what has meant so much to them. They will pay any price, make any sacrifice so that a couple's weekend is the deepest and most meaningful experience of their lives. The team on the weekend of John and Kay Wendt were "beautifully if painfully honest and sincere. We could easily feel their concern and love for us."

A team's purpose is very simple. Step by step they take couples through the whole process of the dialogue technique. They are there to provide the atmosphere, the information and inspiration needed for couples to use the dialogue technique in the most effective way.

A team personally makes each Encounter they give. This surprises some couples. "I saw the teams working very hard on their relationship on the weekend," said John Lyon. "It was an impetus to continue working at times when I might otherwise have wanted to stop."

In the writing periods of the weekend, each of the team couples and the team priest answer the same questions as the couples no matter how many Marriage Encounters they have given. They are there to grow in the same way as the couples making their first weekend; to immerse themselves in their own deepening relationship. In addition, they share themselves in the presentations, making themselves vulnerable to the couples making the weekend. The team is not removed from the struggles or joys that come on the Encounter. They are not there as teachers, but as sharers, willing to follow their decision to grow in love wherever it may lead.

That is why the teams are willing to sacrifice many other enjoyments, to leave home and children every six or eight weeks to share their dialogue with others. They have flown and continue to fly to different parts of the country and the world knowing the yearning for a deeper marital love has no geographical limits. With a passion to give what has so deeply enriched their own lives, a team's ambition is not only to be great in their love for one another, but also to make dialogue available to everyone on the face of this earth. No cost is too great, no distance too far. Long hours of preparation go into each talk team couples share. Phone bills mount as teams keep in touch with couples to whom they have given the gift of dialogue.

There is a tradition in the theater that the show must go on. Encounter teams go one step further—no understudies. Because their sharing is so personal to their relationship, no one can "stand in" for another team. The overwhelming commitment of the team couples really makes me feel very small sometimes.

Nothing stops them. They will do anything to back up their priest and help the couples make a great weekend. Ray and Norma Pawloski were giving a weekend with me which was uneventful through Saturday, if you didn't count the twenty miracles that were happening—the couples' love that was coming more and more alive. Sunday morning when I saw Ray I said, "What in the name of God hit you? Did you and Norma have a fight?" His face was all puffy and so were his hands. He had no idea what caused it. We thought it was some kind of bite. (It turned out afterward to be a penicillin reaction.) It got worse and worse as the morning progressed. Norma and I tried to get him to go to the doctor but they had the last talk in the afternoon and he was determined to give it. He just wouldn't go no matter how much we urged. When he finally got to give the talk his eyes were swollen almost closed, his voice was thick but he gave that talk. He couldn't let his couples down.

The list of heroes is endless—the husband with a fever of 105; the wife who had a baby the day after giving a weekend; the priest who was driven to a weekend on a hot summer day bundled in sweaters and overcoat as he shivered with chills because he didn't want the weekend to be canceled. Vacation days are divided up throughout the year so teams can give Encounters out of town and have Monday to return home. A young cop took a month's leave of absence without pay to take the Encounter to Australia. A teacher and his wife took a salaryless leave of absence for a year, packed up their three children and gave Marriage Encounters in India.

Thousands of couples have been deeply impressed by the caring and faith of the teams. But one priest, Father Thieu Suntjens, recognized the full dimension of their commitment. "I was always looking for the deep sense of brotherhood I thought should be in people," he said. "But I didn't think it existed any more. I was very struck by it on the weekend. I could almost not believe there was so much faith as existed among the team couples and priest I witnessed. I realized there was a new Church springing up."

Many couples recognize that teams have a dignity about their marriage and their relationship that is attractive. The teams were very meaningful to Charlie and Rita Trujillo, who noticed: "They weren't afraid to express their love in front of others—strangers even! I thought about the saying 'See these Christians how they love each other.' Our love was quieter, more private; they were able to share theirs, and that was impressive. It lit a spark of hope and determination in our hearts. Here were living, breathing examples of Christian love. I think 'who they were' spoke more loudly many times than 'what they said.' They made the ideals seem a believable possibility." Yet team couples are regular people. There is nothing different at all about them. They are regular people who have discovered a richness and beauty in their own lives as a result of the dialogue. They give no guidance except in using the dialogue technique; they do not counsel. They share not great ideas thought up by some expert on marriage but the daily, lived, flesh-and-blood experience of their own lives—their attitudes toward and awarenesses of one another, God, the Church, the Sacrament of Matrimony and their responsibility to the world. "They were very human," said Bernadette Ciecuich. "They start talking about themselves and all of a sudden you realize they're just like you."

A similar reaction was expressed by Joanne Sebetic: "I remember thinking this just is not real. A couple was sitting there saying all the things I had thought about and had kept deep inside. I couldn't believe it was happening. I can remember feeling a tremendous excitement and being very anxious to write to Emil because I wanted to get it all out. All of a sudden these people speaking like this gave me the confidence to be open to Emil and speak my heart."

The team's sharing is always meaningful because it is so real and so close to home. Father Russ Sloun expressed a common pre-weekend attitude when he said, "I went expecting to be bored." Anticipating a retreat format and dry catechetical presentations, he had packed a number of books. "I was amazed," he said later. "It wasn't a teaching weekend and the books were never opened. The sharing was personal and intimate. I remember it very well because it really got to me."

"When we first walked in on our weekend, I looked at a team couple there who were so very young, and I wondered what could they tell us about marriage; we had been married so much longer than they had. After the weekend I realized I was free to be myself," is the experience Jeanne La Mar had. "I had always tried to be the best wife that I could be for Don, but I tried so hard to be what he wanted me to be that I really was not being myself."

Yet, in spite of the interest created, the purpose of teams is not to have couples look at *them* but to look at themselves—at one another. They hope all couples will respond as did Mary McDonnell, who said, "I was impressed that the teams kept themselves out of the limelight. They somehow led us to focus just on each other so we weren't even aware of their being there at times. It seemed it was just the two of us."

The worst thing that could be said to a team couple after a presentation is "You gave such a great talk." For the team, it is not words, not a talk, not a performance. It is a sharing—and the only response to a sharing is a further sharing by the couple on the weekend—a sharing, that is, with each other. As long as the attention of the couples who are making the weekend is still on the team, they have missed the point. The team is only a catalyst. A team's reward is the responsiveness of each husband and wife to one another.

Jim and Joan Benjamin said, "We want to deepen our own relationship and we're grateful for the opportunities for joy and peace that each weekend brings us. We hope that through our openness and honesty with each other the couples on the weekend will trust enough to take the risk of really opening up to one another. We want to be so real for couples that they will believe 'The Impossible Dream' is not only possible but actual."

From Frank and Barbara Jelinek: "We try to introduce the couples on the weekend to a joyful way of life that can be led in the everyday realism of the world. We try to make it believable. We want to share our belief that people are unique and important on a humanistic and spiritual level, to create an atmosphere where couples can find all the goodness in each other."

But the couples, important as they are, are not the entire team. The priest rounds it out. Many couples, before they will agree to go on a Marriage Encounter, ask what the role of the priest is. Even though the presence of the priest assures them of the solidity of the experience, they want to be sure they are not going to be preached at. They're afraid it will be churchy.

Actually, the priest is on the team fundamentally for the same reason as the couples: to act as a catalyst of love for the couples. He is there to deepen his own experience of dialogue and to increase his awareness of himself and his relationship to the people of the Church. He has found a way to increase his capacity to love and he wants to share it.

He is there because he loves the Church, which to him is not a building, a structure, a hierarchy, but the people he serves. His whole calling in life is to share the gospel—the good news of salvation. His care for the people he serves brings the more abundant life that Jesus came to offer them. He helps them understand and live by Jesus' words "Love one another as I have loved you."

On the weekend the priest is honestly much more interested in the couples' closeness with one another as husband and wife. He is not there to get them to talk to God, but to get them to talk to one another. He doesn't address himself to Church issues or concerns, morality or theology, but he does speak about what he has discovered in himself as a result of his relationship with the people he serves. Above all, he shows the difference it makes to him personally when the couples grow in their dialogue and their love for one another.

The priest is not on the weekend to change people's attitudes toward priests. If this happens, it happens incidentally. He is there to help couples realize how special they are, to see that they are not ordinary.

By his very humanness and by his realness the priest does open a door for a couple to God in human terms. On a weekend he is not a figure in the pulpit. He is very much like anybody else. He shares the same struggle to be a loving person every day and he can bring across something that is very difficult for couples to understand: the notion of being called to a vocation. Often enough couples do not realize that marriage is a vocation. But they do recognize that priesthood is, and that can help them see themselves with different eyes. Many couples on the weekend come to a fuller awareness of their vocation. "I had some ideas of the priest's role in the Church—that he was to serve us," said Dave Coppi. "Now I know that we have something significant in common: a call to love."

Above all, the priest is there to express his tender, human, personal concern for the love each husband and wife have for one another. The priest is there to answer the unspoken question: "How much do we dare risk?" If a priest who is not even married is so concerned about marriage that he can be so open and spend so much of his priesthood, then couples say, "Maybe we could risk ourselves for each other to a greater degree."

Jan Rigdon summed it up well when she said, "I thought it was priests who had to change. Now I realize that I have to. The priest shows that we are all in this together." The enmeshing of couples and priest as a team is a beautiful thing to see. There are no parts in which the priest alone shares; none in which the couple alone shares. Priests and couples share equally as lovers, expressing their love in different ways.

Sometimes couples coming in on Friday night are not sure what part the priest plays in the weekend. Tom Kearns confesses he was puzzled by the presence of the priest. "I figured he was some kind of psychologist or social worker. Maybe a marriage counselor. During the first presentation I kept looking for his wife."

Many other couples shared similar insights into their changed attitudes toward priests after making a Marriage Encounter. On Friday night Nancy Pauly really could not figure the priest out; he didn't fit her image of a priest. "I guess I had a certain idea of what a priest was," she said. "This man was so real I was just taken off guard. There is so much to him . . . his wanting so much for us to love each other. That is really what I remember so clearly—his desire for us to love each other and to dialogue."

Gerry Genovese also saw a different "priest" than she had come to expect. "On the weekend I learned something about priests," she said. "As I looked at that table at each presentation I did not see the 'priest' I had known all my life. He was not sitting there preaching to me, shaking a finger and handing down some biblical history or even teaching. He was real. He was a little way out. I could not figure him out but I knew I liked him. Every time he opened his mouth, he said something that got me right in my heart. I figured this man has got feelings. He is not just a robot performing duties in the Church someplace; he laughs and he jokes. He was quite a guy—we thought so, from the minute we entered the building. He came out, took our bags and then I found out he was the priest on the weekend. It was such an eyeopener. Now, when I go up to Church, I look at the priest and realize this man does have needs, and he does need Len and I to love him. It has made us so much more aware of the priest as a person and not just as someone performing a role."

It's great to be the team couple or priest on a weekend. On Friday night the couples look at you trying to figure you out, wanting to see what you have to say. They are not too sure about you. By Sunday they are just looking at one another wanting to hear what each other has to say. They have you all figured out.

They like you and are sure of you because they like and are sure of one another. You're great because they're great. What a gift to be part of their love—to be a team at the rebirth of twenty-five couples. Forty-four hours to glory.

CHAPTER IV

The Marriage Encounter Experience

The team is absolutely essential to a Marriage Encounter, but as the ignition, not as the engine. The couple is the engine. The team doesn't attempt to tell the couple new things but to trigger self-recognition in them, while encouraging them to share that self-awareness with their spouse. This focus gives the Marriage Encounter weekend a special dynamic not found on most retreats. When someone goes on a retreat and the retreat master is great, then it was a great retreat. However, the experience fades and in a couple of days or a couple of weeks, it is all over. The person has lost it.

You can't take the retreat master home with you, but, in a way, on a Marriage Encounter you can. Because really the team does not give the Encounter. The couple give the Encounter to one another. What the team points out is how to go about it, what to avoid and what they have experienced as a result of their practice of dialogue. Nobody, though, can practice dialogue for the couple except the couple. So when they leave at the end of a Marriage Encounter weekend, they have everything because they have each other. Now, they have the way to discover each other more fully. So after an Encounter they don't have anything new. What they have is a way to see what was already there and has always been there, plus, through continuing dialogue, a way to continue to grow in love. Marriage Encounter helps each couple recognize their own beauty. Most couples arrive on the weekend believing they are just another couple. What is taken away by Sunday is the word "just." We assume no couple is ordinary, and if we can only give them a sense of their specialness on the weekend, we have gone a long way toward achieving our goal.

Nancy Grella puts it this way: "Our weekend showed me how much I really do love Mike and how special we are as a couple. We had always put ourselves down. We're standing in a new light; we really see ourselves now as good people. Being more for each other every day."

So Marriage Encounter doesn't make people better, it merely creates the occasion where people become aware of the richness they already have. It's like the experience of the kid who has just hit a home run and stands stunned at the plate. What he is really saying is, "I didn't know I had it in me." Couples come home from an Encounter weekend looking at one another and just saying, "We didn't know we had it in us."

A fairly typical love story is about the boy and girl who grew up next door to each other and never noticed one another. She was just another girl until one day she became *the* girl. She still had those freckles; now he loved freckles. She was still a motor mouth; but now that motor purred.

Before she was a girl; now for him she is *my* girl. What happened was that before he *saw* her; now he *noticed* her. Before he *heard* her; now he *listened* to her. Nothing had really changed in her; he had changed in the way he looked at her. Now he was paying attention to her. The most fascinating part of this whole thing is that as soon as he gets involved with her, she becomes *his*. It is not a possessive type of thing, but a being part of him. It really says more about whom *he* belongs to than it does about her. He wouldn't say *my* girl before. Not because of what it would say about her, but because of what it would commit him to.

Marriage Encounter makes the *my* in "my wife," "my husband" very strong. It doesn't say she belongs to me; it says I belong to her. It leads me to pay real attention, to truly listen, to fully notice. It doesn't get the other person to change; it changes how I see that person.

We've been living not next door to one another, but in the same house with each other for a number of years. Marriage Encounter helps us to look at one another. One Friday evening a very fussy, portly couple drove up in an El Dorado. The couple had obviously gone to the right schools, lived in the right neighborhood and associated with the right people. They were quite self-contained and proper. He was quite satisfied with himself and very proud of her, much as he was of his Cadillac. When he introduced her, he said that she was a lady. She obviously was. They had a difficult weekend because he had to reverse the pattern of a lifetime and concentrate on the two of them as persons rather than on getting ahead and what he could do for her. They were great though. They kept struggling. They worked like dogs. On Sunday he had his arm around her and said to everyone "She's *my* lady"—she obviously was.

Couples always attest to finding more within themselves than they ever dreamed they had. The qualities and beauty uncovered in the search are as diverse as the people who come to the weekend. But always there is that "something special" for each individual husband and wife:

"I learned that I was free to be myself," Mike Beattie reported. "I even felt if I said something silly or tender I wouldn't receive any backlash."

"Ken's faithfulness to our relationship was affirmed again and again on the weekend," said Patty Rowell. "He always brings hope to our relationship."

"We were going along, we were happy, great. But there was something missing," Joe Marchese said. "The tension would build up over a couple of months, then we would blow up and then things would be better because it would bring us together again. But we could not figure out what the heck was wrong. We did not have a handle on our marriage. I guess what we found out on our weekend was a way to feel close every day. It removed the aimless wandering we had had in our marriage. We were given a direction."

In talking with people all over the country about the results of Marriage Encounter, "aware" was a frequently used word. The use of the dialogue technique makes couples aware of one another and gives them a tool for continued growth in love, what Don Capretta referred to as "a way to keep our awareness of each other sharp."

Phil Coffey expressed what most couples seem to be saying: "On the weekend I became aware I had something to offer. I realized what I could do isn't as important as who I am. I also realized I had to work to make our marriage better. I had always thought we'd have a good marriage just because that was what we wanted."

"To me our Marriage Encounter was the one most significant experience of my life," was the statement of Hugo Van Dijck. "It opened up a complete new dimension in our coupleness. I thought we had a good marriage before, but it became very clear we had moments when there was a great chasm between us. On the weekend, when we were asked to look for the selfishness and lack of responsiveness and lack of communication with one another, I realized I was always finding Lisa's selfishness and not my own. After that I tried to listen to her and not to myself."

Those comments may seem obvious, and any thinking person would agree, but it is amazing how these truths do not come alive in our day-to-day living. All too often in marriage, couples look without seeing, they hear without listening—too busy. "People in general seem to be living in the same house day after day but never seem to be truly married. Every day you must make the decision to be married," is the way Catherine Holt expressed an insight she received on the weekend.

Let's look at a typical scene in the day of a couple. The guy gets up in the morning, jumps into his pants, grabs a quick cup of coffee, shaves, rushes off to catch the 7:03. She gets up, gives the kids breakfast, dresses them, gets them off to school, cleans the house, does the laundry, takes out the cleaning, does the shopping and prepares the dinner. He gets in on the

6:38, takes a quick look at the mail. They sit down to eat and spend the meal getting the rundown on the children's activities, what Johnny did at Cub Scouts, what Mary has for homework, why Timmy is crying. After supper, they load the dishwasher and start the kids on their homework. He might take forty winks on the couch, read the newspaper or watch television. In snatches they discuss the activities of their day. Then the kids have to be bathed, pajamaed and settled down in bed. They have to unwind from the storm of bedtime for the kids. There may be a few chores still to be done. About the only time they really have a chance to talk to each other is when they go to bed at night and, by that time, they are too worn out to talk about anything other than some kind of a pressing problem, concern or upset. Pat Berrigan shared a personal experience along those lines: "Barbara and I would rarely talk to each other on a regular basis before Marriage Encounter. We would get together when situations reached crisis proportions, but then we would generally argue. At other times our conversation was pretty superficial."

When does the couple really have a chance to talk to each other? On weekends? Then they seem to have the most time, but really it adds up to the least time with one another. It is filled with the swirl of Little League and dancing class, Confraternity of Christian Doctrine and church, football games and television, family outings and visiting the relatives.

Actually, there is frequently more talking to one another Monday through Thursday than there is on the weekend. Ask any couple, "When was the last chance you took to sit and talk to one another about each other?" Many will find they are like Ethel and Bob Reber: "The timing had to be right for both Bob and I," Ethel said. "We talked about lots of things, even about our childhood, analyzing how our attitudes were formed. But before dialogue we never really spoke 'us.' Before dialogue we often *talked* but we rarely were absorbed in listening to understand and really hear the plea for comfort, love, understanding."

The weekend changes this picture. It is amazing how some time together spent in dialogue creates an atmosphere of openness and trust. Sometimes there are some very stark realizations, such as that of George Hess. "Friday night I turned them off, fell asleep, thought it was all a bunch of . . . On Sunday it hit me, I fell in love with Toni."

Tom Healy said, "Our Marriage Encounter was the first time in ten years we paid attention to each other for a solid forty-four hours. I told my sister we thought we had a great marriage. But we paid attention to kids, house, hobbies, cars, and we fit each other in when it was convenient."

"We decided to make a Marriage Encounter weekend because we were dissatisfied with our relationship as it existed," said Bill and Margie Beal. "We both had a longing to be closer to each other and be able to talk freely with each other. We seemed to explode at each other over nothing (unimportant irritations), for example, who left the car on empty, who used all the toothpaste and forgot to replace it, why weren't there any towels in the bathroom when I finished my shower, etc. We both knew this was meaningless trivia, but didn't know how to help ourselves stop these harmful discussions. On the weekend we truly became aware of each other as good human beings, who were very special to one another. We discovered we existed for each other because that was what we really wanted, not because we were a convenience to one another."

How easily said, "I just want to be me," yet, so difficult. For Tom Kearns the obstacle was "a lot of self-imposed restrictions. Once I was freed from them," he said, "it provided almost a daily opportunity to give more for Mary and the kids, myself, God and just about everyone I came in contact with. I had thought people, including Mary, expected certain things from me. All the things I thought people needed, I automatically tried to provide. On the weekend I learned I don't have to be so concerned about meeting expectations, but I do have to let Mary see the real me."

Other couples had similar freeing experiences on the weekend.

For Madeleine Chicavich it was breaking out of routine: "Marriage Encounter returned us to the beauty that had been us." And for Jan Tolfa: "Coupleness is a whole new world. It seemed amazing we never thought of opening up more before. The rewards are so great; it's worth anything you have to do to get it."

Marriage Encounter says "hallelujah" to the popular song "I've Got to Be Me." But it also says that there should be a sequel to that song: "We've Got to Be Us." On a Marriage Encounter weekend there are couples of every age and circumstance who are repeating the same refrain. The call of a couple is to love one another. They can't fully love one another just by doing good things for one another and adding snatches of sexual intimacy.

Marriage is a total relationship in which the full awareness of one another is reveled in, appreciated and developed to the deepest possible degree each day.

"My new awarenesses of Mike were like being thrown into cold water to be awakened," said Nancy Grella. "It's like waking up every day and saying, no matter what kind of day it is, I'm going to put him first. At times it's very difficult. But I know that if we are going to have a good day, I'm going to have to decide to be open to him. By trusting enough to be open, we are able to grow much closer."

But the exciting result of this "awareness" of themselves and each other in the couples is the *hope* couples begin to experience. Probably the greatest contribution that the Marriage Encounter experience offers any couple is hope. So often a couple will say their happiest days were when they first met, fell in love, got married. That really is not our Heavenly Father's plan for us. His plan for us is that the happiest moment in our life is *now*.

The hope comes in many forms. Ralph Florio sees that he responds to his wife differently now: "We just see each other so much more now. We're starting to look at not only the big things. It's the subtle things." John Saabye is amazed at himself: "You wouldn't believe the changes, because I hardly believe them myself. We have spent more time married in the last six months than we have for fifteen years. I don't need clubs, or activities, or whiskey any more—I have Joan."

The hope generated on the weekend is born in the knowledge that God's plan for marriage is for couples to revel in the joy of love. When Jesus said, "I tell you these things that my joy may be in you and your joy may be complete" (John 15:11), He did not imply that common attitude about the will of God which says that if it is good it must be unpleasant, if not outright painful. What becomes clear is that the world's plan for marriage, while promising so much happiness, leaves us with the great pain of loneliness and misunderstanding. When couples with good marriages watch contentment grow into complacency and glimpses of happiness flower into possessiveness and jealousy. A nagging discontent creeps in. "There has got to be more" they realize; like the words of Peggy Lee's song, they ask: "Is That All There Is?"

Mike Grella told his wife Nancy, "There is something behind this. It didn't meet my eye right off the bat and it scared me for a minute." What Mike saw is that Marriage Encounter is an attempt to try God's way. It is an act of faith in a belief that greatness for a couple is for a husband to turn to his wife and say, "I am going to listen to you right now, better than you have ever been listened to in your whole life"; for a wife to turn to her husband and say, "I am going to make you feel you are the most understood man in the world; I am going to use all the powers of my concentration, all the love of which I am capable strictly and solely to focus in on understanding you now."

Marriage Encounter asks a couple merely to say I am going to find myself, and I am going to help you find yourself. I am going to share the self I find fully and totally without reservation with you, and I am going to reach out to accept the self you discover and share with me totally without reservation. It holds out to a couple the opportunity to change their priorities and to stop putting each other behind all sorts of other aims and goals in life.

The technique of dialogue, and resulting closeness of relationship, offers the couple the chance to be lovers—and it takes little imagination to see that this is a call to greatness, for the whole world needs love. A couple says to each other, "I am going to share the self that I find fully and totally without reservation with you. I am going to reach out to accept the self that you discover and share with me as completely as I can." Then the seeds of a cosmic rebirth are sown—the plan of God, seen at the moment of creation and the final trumpet and summed up in a word—*love*—without qualification or limit—from the truest depth of our being. Marriage Encounter gives couples an opportunity to dare to be different. It is a chance to find the greatness that is within every marriage simply by living it fully. Through the dialogue technique come flashes of the potential for greatness that is planted in every one of us. The greatness is not in what we can accomplish and what our talents are, or what our capabilities may be. The greatness is us and our capability to be lovers.

CHAPTER V

Feelings

As the Marriage Encounter weekend progresses many different aspects of marriage are discussed. One of the key subjects is feelings, and much of what is shared is a distillation of our own lived experience. Many of the insights have been joyous, but some were born in pain. We learned a great deal about feelings on a weekend I now think of as our "Good Friday."

In April 1970 we had a training weekend for our teams. I was really looking forward to a great weekend. This was an open sharing weekend, and we started out by telling everyone we wanted them to share their feelings without any holding back for fear of being criticized or judged. After all, it is one of our principles that feelings are neither right nor wrong so no one could quarrel with any feeling shared. They could feel perfectly free with any feeling.

There were several couples making this team training who were already teams. Almost from the start of the weekend some of them had a very difficult time. Their struggle and pain was evident to all. We discovered later they had been sometimes substituting Encounter work for their own dialogue, in spite of a commitment each had made to use the dialogue in building their relationship each day. If they talked a lot about dialogue or the Encounter on a given evening either with each other or with other Marriage Encounter couples they often excused themselves from their own daily dialogue. So when they began this weekend with its focus on putting their own coupleness first they saw how foolish they had been. It hurt them very much to realize they had been teachers of dialogue to others but hadn't been using it themselves.

The atmosphere remained heavy until Saturday afternoon when one of the wives told the group she was going to make a banner to symbolize this weekend. The words on it would be "Love Is a Kick in the Ass." Her ability to laugh at herself gave everyone hope and a little laughter broke up the clouds in the room. Our spirits lifted and morale began to pick up.

On Sunday morning another couple stood up and admitted they had discovered their "little church" (meaning their own coupleness) was in ruins but they were going to tear it down and build a cathedral. All of us were moved by their honesty and their vision.

Then it happened—a beautiful young couple, wonderfully idealistic, stood up after lunch with something they had to say. They felt we were all a bunch of phonies, tearing down little churches and building cathedrals. (They thought the older teams were saying these things in order to get the newer teams to share more deeply on the weekend.) I was dumbstruck, I knew in my heart they were wrong; and even if they had been correct it would have been wrong for them to say it. But I was struck with the remembrance of my own pleading on Friday night asking couples to share their feelings without fear of comment since feelings couldn't be judged.

The atmosphere in the room turned cold and dark. We stumbled through Mass, muttered good-byes to one another and got out as fast as we could. Driving home I thought to myself, "It isn't worth all this pain. We can't do this to such good people. This feeling business is too dangerous." Then the thunderbolt struck me. That wasn't a feeling. What that young couple said wasn't a feeling at all. It was a judgment. Feelings don't tear us apart but judgments do.

Good Friday does lead to Easter Sunday. Everything we now share on a Marriage Encounter about feelings and discovering them within ourselves is based on the events of that April weekend.

Unless we have made a Marriage Encounter or had a similar experience, many of us make the same mistake as the couple on that team training weekend. We express our "feelings" in the form of strongly held opinions or judgments with a thinly veiled anger or upset behind our words.

Part of the difficulty we experience in sharing feelings is that there normally isn't a clear distinction in conversation between feelings, thoughts and judgments. *I feel* and *I think* are used pretty much interchangeably. The only difference is *I feel* is more often used when the opinion is weak or there are strong feelings behind the statement. For example, "I feel that the kids are going to be good today" really is a thought and it cannot be proved. There are feelings of hopefulness behind it and perhaps some fear it won't happen. Or we might say, "I feel that we should spend our vacation away this year." Again, this is a judgment rather than a feeling, but behind it there may well be feelings of boredom from the remembrance of the last at-home vacation. "I feel you spend too much time with the children" or "I feel you are absorbed in your job" are other examples. There again, very strong feelings underlie the judgments made in those statements: feelings of sadness and loneliness, and, underneath those, desire and yearning.

Most couples who come on an Encounter weekend don't even know they are not talking about feelings with one another. They use the word and use it frequently, but what they are really doing is stating a position. Take, for example, the man who says to his wife that he feels she is spending too much time with the kids. She tends to answer along the lines of how much attention she pays to him; she defends the time with the kids on the basis that they need it and, after all, they are only little tots and he can wait. She explains she really much prefers to spend time with him but, after all, she has a responsibility to the children and he should understand. If his tone in making the statement has been harsh, she is liable to attack and say he is just being selfish; if he spent more time with the kids then maybe she wouldn't have to spend so much. So the conclusion of this whole thing might well be a rip-roaring fight. In the end, he might feel a little bit better because he got it off his chest, or she might decide to try to stretch herself a little bit more and give him some extra attention.

What happened, though, was that she heard his complaint, his judgment on her; she didn't hear his heart. She heard those words and what those words meant. She didn't hear it all—his feelings of distance, coldness and loneliness.

The same thing can happen the other way. She can tell him she feels his job is more important to him than she is. Once again that is not a feeling; that is her judgment, but it is based on her yearning for him or on a desire to be close to him. He too hears only her words, the judgment she is making, and he will respond accordingly. He can tell her he would love to spend more time with her, but that doesn't put food on the table. He can tell her he is working hard for her and for the kids. Depending on how she made the original statement and whether he is feeling upset himself or not, he might become very defensive and tell her she is lucky to have it so easy while he has all the worries. Once again the resolution might be just a palliative in which he decides for a few weeks to come home a little bit earlier from the office and maybe not make so many business phone calls when he does get home. Or she might agree with him that her "feeling" was wrong.

When we mix the two—our judgments and feelings—and try to talk about them simultaneously, we have problems. But it is very common to confuse them because few of us have had very much experience in sharing feelings. We don't know how to express them; and we don't know how to listen when they are shared.

Rita Gorremans of Antwerp, expressed a problem many of us have, "Having been used to giving my opinions all the time, it was difficult for me to separate them from feelings. Nor was I enthusiastic about expressing my feelings to Jean. I preferred to limit myself to thoughts and judgments; they were much more evident to me than my feelings."

What is being offered through Marriage Encounter is a deeper dimension to marriage. It is couples with good relationships who come on Marriage Encounter. They have built their relationship through frequent deep and attentive interchanges of ideas, thoughts, concepts and dreams. But their awareness of feelings has, in all likelihood, been more limited. Over the years they have talked over opinions, have made a lot of plans and know each other's capabilities and talents; but they have probably shared feelings only incidentally. Because we neglect feelings in our society, very few if any couples have shared feelings to the degree they share them on a Marriage Encounter.

Usually the realization that feelings have been shoved aside comes as a surprise. As an example, Seamus O'Donohoe said, "I thought there were no flaws in our relationship; but I realized on the weekend there was a part of us which we hadn't been tuned into very much at all."

It is difficult for some couples to understand why feelings are so important. Because they talk often, they think they know each other inside and out.

Many couples, prior to Encounter, are like the Hendersons: "After knowing her for fourteen years, I pretty much knew what Sheila thought and how she would react in most situations," Carl said. "In fact a lot of our conversation could be completed by half sentences and gestures, like a pointed finger, a frown or a knowing glance. But I knew only a few of her feelings."

Though we may think we know each other well, when we neglect feelings in a relationship, we neglect the deepest, most intimate part of ourselves. Our thinking process can be shared with anyone; but our feelings can be shared only with someone we trust deeply. We have no particular control over our feelings; they come and go seemingly at will. We can increase them or we can damp them down a little bit. We can even set ourselves up for certain feelings, but in fact most feelings just come. Feelings are like the color of one's hair. They are simply part of the experience of being one's self.

Since there is no morality attached to feelings—they are neither right nor wrong—we have the freedom to enjoy them in each other. This leads us to great closeness because feelings are very personal, the most intimate part of us. The sharing of a deep feeling is the greatest gift a human being can give to another. An equally tremendous gift of love is reaching out for the feelings of another person, not in order to console him or make him feel differently, but simply to taste the experience of that person—to stand in his shoes. What is important about feelings is that they are personal. What is important about thoughts is that they are correct. Everyone is interested in something that is correct or makes sense. The only person interested in feelings is someone who cares.

That is not to say, of course, a relationship should be built solely on feelings, for that would be a very narrow and limited one. But it *is* saying that feelings are a very intimate, real and important part of us, and one far too often neglected in conversation. A relationship that is alive, vibrant and close is built more on the experience of each other's feelings than on any other single factor. Without a deep awareness of feelings, a relationship is crippled.

It isn't hard for many of us to relate to the experience of Anne Roney: "Our life together was in a sense only half a life because I seldom expressed or even thought about my feelings. This resulted in my dropping 'clues' in hopes that Hugh would notice I was upset and understand why. What was so frustrating was that the 'clues' were rarely picked up, and I didn't know where to go from there. Also, I would guess at how Hugh felt and respond to him on the basis of my guesses. Often, my response was more likely to be a change in my actions than a sharing. And I never knew for sure if my guesses were right or wrong."

Others can understand the kind of rut John Brendese described: "We had reached the stage in our marriage where we tended to hold things back in order not to rock the boat. Without intending for it to happen, walls were going up, and we didn't know what to do. We had been so busy with social commitments, raising a family, all the different aspects of daily living that we never slowed up to really think about *how* to communicate."

Others, like Joan Rizzo, thought it was best to avoid the negative. "Just prior to our Marriage Encounter," Joan said, "I was trying to concentrate on being very positive by ignoring whatever I saw that seemed negative, especially in myself. I didn't think Bernard wanted to hear how I was feeling when I was 'down,' and when I first heard about sharing feelings, I got a little uptight. My immediate reaction was that it was best to keep up a positive front."

Not only do we often fail to share our feelings with those close to us, but often, because we do not really know ourselves, we fail to recognize our feelings. Like Bieke Soenens, whom I met in Antwerp, Belgium, we *think* we know ourselves, but when we take more time and search more deeply, we find we were wrong. "I knew only general feelings, just the feelings on the surface," said Bieke. "I had been analyzing myself, looking for facts and reasons to explain my feelings. Often I turned to the past looking for an answer. But this didn't really help me or bring me any closer to my husband. Also, he seldom really shared himself with me. Although he would tell me there were no deep feelings there, I couldn't accept that. I was curious about the *real* Raf; I was longing for a real partner."

This getting beyond the surface feeling that Bieke speaks of is vital to knowing ourselves and one another; and on a Marriage Encounter couples are urged to discover the feelings, underneath those they recognize first. Most couples have shared some feelings. For instance, anger and even hurt might commonly be shared. But anger and hurt are to my real emotions what pain is to appendicitis. Pain is a clue to the doctor, a symptom of something deeper. The same is true with anger or hurt. They are a tip-off to us that something is churning around down deep within us. It may be a loneliness, a fear, a desire, or what have you. On a Marriage Encounter we ask couples to search for the real feelings behind those we often notice.

Even in small matters, it might be only the surface feelings that are expressed. For instance, Tommie Ennis told me "If Ann appeared in a new rig-out, I felt pleased and excited that she looked so attractive, but I would say, 'How much did it cost?' because my feelings of insecurity were given first voice. My strong basic feelings of insecurity and shyness prevented my feelings of admiration and pleasure from finding expression, and Ann saw only the resentment. Another time there was a row at work that upset me a lot. Ann knew only the irritability that was so evident. Since I thought the problem didn't really concern Ann, I didn't share it; so she knew nothing of my fears and anxieties yet she suffered from my sour disposition."

In our society, men are trained from the time they are small boys that feelings are for girls. They learn that boys don't cry; men don't wear their hearts on their sleeves. A man learns to expect himself to be strong at all times; a show of feelings is considered a sign of weakness. Even anger—about the only feeling men are allowed to show—is preferably kept hidden. Men are afraid to display any of the gentler feelings for fear their manhood will be questioned. How many men are even able to cry at the funeral of a parent or a wife?

To show how men bury certain feelings, let's look at a man driving along on a highway when a car swerves in front of him. Quite naturally, he gets a clamp of fear in his stomach. The feeling of fear is not a weakness; it is a normal reaction to danger. Then, as the danger passes, his fear gives way to anger, which is actually an expression of the relief he feels now that the danger is past. Later he emphasizes the anger and bitterness he felt rather than the fear and relief, because he judges the former, probably unconsciously, to be more appropriate feelings for a man to have. He sees the fear as a momentary weakness. A man believes he should avoid feelings or ignore them. They attack his image of manliness. "I looked at feelings as being unmanly," Patrick McGilloway said. "I thought they were something to be covered up, so whenever I had feelings, I'd try to avoid them. The feelings I noticed most were those of desire—feelings with temptations attached to them—and I wanted to escape and overcome them. It hit me like a ton of bricks to be told that feelings were neither right nor wrong. It gave me a sense of freedom."

Because most men have virtually no practice in expressing emotions, some have a difficult time at the beginning of the Marriage Encounter weekend. Team couples always urge both partners to be gentle, kind and patient. Wally Wallace shared his Friday night struggles in a rap session with friends: "I didn't think I had any feelings at all when we were told the focus of the Encounter. I thought I was an unemotional, analytical person, and I didn't want to express feelings or even face them, except when it came to showing my love for Dot. Ever since I was a kid, I was discouraged from showing emotion. I was told to be strong. My father never hugged or kissed me; he always shook my hand. He wanted us to be rough and tough. It seemed so masculine to live up to my image of my father that I even wanted to prove my manliness to Dot. Even when I cared, I didn't want others to see it. Often this caused me to seem distant and cold. It was hard for me to get into the weekend. Gradually I was able to open up, but at first I was confused and upset."

Although women are permitted more freedom in expressing feelings, even they learn to conceal many of their deeper feelings, not wanting to be thought naïve or weak. Also, implied in the freedom women are allowed in expressing feelings is the unfortunate judgment that their greater tendency to let emotions show, somehow makes them less than men, that their feelings make them unreliable or fickle. Furthermore, we still limit the feelings women can freely express. Some feelings are not considered proper for women to have. "I always thought there were certain feelings that were okay and others that were wrong," said Nancy Finn. "If I had a bad feeling—one I thought was wrong— I felt trapped when I couldn't get rid of it." "I had four feelings —good, not so good, tired and okay," Sandy Atkinson said. "Everything else stayed inside."

Another way we often get trapped into sex roles in communicating is by thinking that while women are allowed to have feelings, the job of the man in her life is to make her feel better. To take those feelings away from her. Often both men and women are guilty of trying to convince another person to change a feeling because we think it is inappropriate or upsetting or inconvenient or unrealistic. When we do this, we encourage others to bury their feeling. We sometimes also get involved in activities or encourage others to do so to escape or avoid facing a feeling. "I never understood why Joan would stop talking when I'd try to change feelings like sadness—to try to help her feel 'better,'" said Art Flaherty, describing how he used to act. As a result "we'd end up walking away from each other. I would fume inside and Joan would call her sister or a friend."

Too often husbands and wives live together for years without knowing each other's feelings. Husbands might excuse themselves by thinking, "Women are different. Who can understand them?" Wives say, "I know my husband like a book." Unfortunately, the same result comes from both statements: a failure to reach out and really experience and enjoy the other person.

Rather sadly, you hear husbands and wives who have been married a number of years admit to a certain boredom or apathy setting in. They recognize that there was something special about the dating years and early years of marriage. They haven't really experienced the same since except maybe in tiny little snatches. They recognize they can't live in a world of romance and that they have built so much between them over the years they didn't have then, but there is a certain regret in their hearts. Where has that specialness gone? They had such feeling for one another, they were so very responsive to one another's joys and sorrows.

Now they talk mostly about things: money, kids, house, job, vacations. They think they know all there is to know about each other when actually they are missing the real uniqueness of each other. For, "sharing feelings brings excitement," as Ann Gilbert learned. "Ken and I used to try to fit ourselves into the kind of suit we thought a good husband or wife should wear," she said. "But we missed the feelings that make us who we are."

In our lifetime we don't come up with many new ideas. We don't do that many different things on a given day, or even over the course of a year. But each day of our lives our feelings change; in any situation they make us special and unique. Tom Heffernan said, "Eileen and I were married thirty-nine years, yet on our weekend we learned much that was new about each other —feelings we'd held back."

A rather typical scene in most homes is the man coming home from work in the afternoon. His wife greets him at the door with "What's new?" Frequently he answers "Nothing." Actually she is asking the wrong question. What she wants is some news to entertain her to know who is going with whom; who is getting a divorce; who is being promoted; what exciting thing happened around the office. But these are commonplace events for him, and he takes them in stride. He has no interest in them. Perhaps he does mention something that happened around the office which leads into a conversation about who did what, whether it was right or not, what they would do in the circumstances, how it affects them and so forth and so on. But there is nothing really personal about this. The real question should be "What's new with *you?* How are you feeling right now? It doesn't matter whether it was some interesting event that caused the feeling, it is just *you* and *your* feeling which are important to me." What the Marriage Encounter weekend offers is a sensitivity to how I am feeling and a willingness to share this with my spouse. Marriage Encounter reveals the importance of feelings and a freedom to express them. Not only does it offer motivation and show the importance of sharing feelings between husband

and wife, but it actually gives a technique whereby we can go on doing it. It is the technique we call dialogue.

The real beauty of dialogue is that it is a nonjudgmental form of communication. It centers around sharing and experiencing feelings. In every other form of communication, judgment is involved. We evaluate the ideas offered, we analyze the actions and reactions in the events described to us. We consider various alternatives and select among them or we listen to hear who in our own judgment is right and who is wrong. In dialogue there is no right or wrong. There is no problem to be solved, no decision to be made and therefore the issue is not the issue. We are not trying to formulate a decision or a plan, only to come to a greater awareness of each other. Luke McSherry found "it was like pulling a cork and allowing me to be me by telling me that feelings were neither good nor bad." No matter how much pressure we put on a man or woman, or even on ourselves, not to have feelings or to have only certain feelings, the feelings are there. Until we face the reality of their presence, we can never be free.

We are constantly evaluating our feelings and judging ourselves by our feelings. Therefore, on a Marriage Encounter weekend, there is a tremendous release when it is emphasized that feelings are neither right nor wrong, they just *are*. Accepting that as truth, helps us not only to discover our own feelings but to accept the feelings of others. "I can't say I didn't know how my wife felt before we began to dialogue," Phil Doucette said. "Her feelings showed on her face and in her actions." But, like so many of us, Phil didn't know how to respond to feelings. "I'd start making judgments about her because she had certain feelings, or I would try to perk her up. I'd wonder what I'd done to cause her feelings; and I'd focus on my own actions."

So often when feelings come up in a conversation, our instantaneous reaction is to ask *why*—why do you feel that way? Then the conversation shifts to the causes, and the feelings get lost.

Frequently feelings are rejected; people are told they "shouldn't feel that way." But in dialogue, we don't have to explain, we don't have to defend, we don't have to excuse. A feeling—yours or mine—is simply accepted and shared. Time and time again Encountered couples report the dialogue technique releases them to be whole; it takes off the strait-jacket. How wonderful to know someone else really cares how—and that—you feel.

Yet for all the joy couples experience from the sharing of feelings, it isn't easy to do. Because feelings are so intimate and personal, sharing them with someone else, even with a spouse, leaves us vulnerable to that person. It is a lot easier to say to someone "You did such and such a thing, and I didn't like it. I would like you to change." Saying "I feel hurt" is harder; it leaves us open to rejection or attack. When we express thoughts and opinions, we are not personally on the line; when we express feelings, we are. If we describe our thoughts and they aren't accepted, we can always try another one. If, however, I share my feelings with you and you reject them or try to change them, then you are rejecting me as a person—who I am—and that is a lot harder to take. That is why we often avoid deep feelings; we fear the possible rejection or we fear being judged or misunderstood. Sharing feelings also threatens our independence. We sense that it ties us too much to another person, and we back away. Being open to Jim with her feelings was difficult for Mary Pat Toner. "There is a freedom and lightness in being vulnerable to one another. But I fear revealing certain feelings I'd rather keep to myself. I tell myself I don't want to be a burden to Jim, or I want to enjoy my moods and can revel in them without talking about how I feel, or I'm afraid that he won't like seeing me as a weak person or a fearful one." Yet, because of the vulnerability in sharing feelings, having them accepted by someone else gives us a greater freedom and lightness than any other kind of communication. It brings us to the greatest possible closeness.

Al Regnier discovered "a whole 99 per cent of Barbara I never knew before. She was giving me something I could keep. Even if I physically held her, she could be mine for only so long. But when she shared herself—her deepest feelings—with me, she gave me something of her I could keep forever."

CHAPTER VI

The Technique of Dialogue

At this writing every Friday night sixty-five Encounters begin around the world. The chairs are all arranged for from twenty to twenty-five couples who will be making the weekend. On each chair rests a notebook and pen. Very prosaic, isn't it? Yet that is where it all begins—in those notebooks. They are the do-it-yourself kit for a couple on a Marriage Encounter weekend.

At the end of every presentation the team asks each husband and wife to go quietly off alone and pour into that little notebook the feelings they have within them.

Over the period of years in a marriage a lot of dust gets spread over the bright shiny wedding gown, and couples tend to lose sight of the specialness they once had in their spouse's eyes. Marriage Encounter offers the opportunity to rejuvenate that specialness, bring back the sparkle and dust off the wedding dress; it makes couples walk ten feet tall. Nobody gave them their specialness when they first met; they discovered it in one another. Likewise, nobody in Marriage Encounter is going to give them that specialness; they have to discover it again in themselves. The way they discover it is through the dialogue technique of writing and sharing their writing with one another. The Marriage Encounter theme song is "I'll Never Find Another You." By the time couples get to the end of the weekend they are singing it with fervor and with the deepest heart-felt meaning.

In the beginning, at least, many object, sometimes strenuously, to the writing. The team has to work very hard at convincing all the couples of the absolute necessity of putting pen to paper.

"My reaction was I wanted to get out of the bloody place," said Joe Donnelly, who later said he "got used to writing feelings and wouldn't give it up." Despite initial reluctance like Joe's to writing on the weekend, my faith in the writing is great. I believe with all my heart if it's just tried it works every time for every couple.

One weekend a young couple wasn't getting into the weekend. They wouldn't co-operate in any way. After each presentation they went up to their room and didn't even try to write. He was hostile; she was afraid of him. I saw their weekend going down the drain, so I went up to him and asked him to give it a chance. "Look," he replied, "I'm a flat-out kind of a guy. If I want to say something, I say it. I don't need to write." He pushed by me and went to his room.

It went on like that through Saturday night until just before supper when I heard music blaring from their room. They were noticeably embarrassed and turned down the radio when I pointed out the distraction it was causing other couples. I then told them they were just throwing away their own Encounter. "Say," he blurted, "what those dames are getting away with [referring to the sharing of couples]; if any broad did that to me I'd deck 'em." This was it. Obviously, he wasn't going to move. I figured there wasn't any hope the way we were going; what did we have to lose. I'd have my best shot. He was standing there a little bantam of a guy, his shirt open, the hair popping out on his chest. I said to him, "The trouble with you is that you're trying to live up to being an Italian man." With that he took a step toward me, when in a very weak voice she said, "You're right." He stopped as if he had been poleaxed. It was obviously the first time in their marriage she had ever spoken up to him. I looked at her and told her, "You know what you have to do? You have to start a rip-roaring fight." She said, "I know. But I'm scared."

After supper for the first time they started to write. Sunday they came up with a big smile as they were leaving hand in hand. Rather shyly, he said, "I don't think we got the full experience while we were here, could we come back?" Three weeks later they returned. After a great weekend, he convinced twelve builders from his construction crew friends to make an Encounter.

As that couple learned, it is a very exhilarating experience to sit down with a cheap little copy book and a pen and all of a sudden discover that the pen is mightier than the mouth, that actually there is a tremendous amount of wealth and richness inside us that we have lived with all our lives and never recognized.

There are many persuasive reasons why writing is part of a Marriage Encounter, but most important is that in dialogue we are sharing feelings. Most of us have had very little experience in even defining what a feeling is, much less discovering it within ourselves and recognizing the full dimensions of it.

Feelings can be rather gossamer-like things. Unless we put them down on paper, they can slip away without our even knowing we have lost them. When we are talking it is easy to shorthand or undersell our feelings. It is not easy to talk only about feelings, especially when we are trying to recognize the feelings underneath the surface. It is so easy in conversation to settle for noticing just the symptoms. But we usually bring a greater intensity to our writing and, therefore, have a sharper eye for what is really going on inside of us.

John and Maryann Toohil expanded on the advantages of writing. "From what John wrote, I realized he loves me for what I am and not because I fit an image," Maryann said. "Recognizing this, I began to see myself in a different light. I saw him taking a risk by sharing and making me a more important part of his life, and I found myself wanting to return the same trust. It was a scary experience, but it was beautiful. John's writing and his openness encouraged me and helped *me* to be more open. I figured if he could do it, I could too. At first it seemed very risky. Now I realize how much I had held back from John. I don't think I was seeing him as he really was before the weekend. When we talked, I heard only those things that fit my image of him. Actually, it was the atmosphere of the entire weekend that helped us deepen our relationship; but the writing was a big part of it."

"The writing made us both want to share in a way we had never shared before," John added. "We thought we had been very open with each other; but here was a whole new focus. I had never really described feelings. Sharing them was like falling in love all over again. I seemed to be discovering a whole new person as I read Maryann's notebook. There were sides to her I'd never known existed, even though I always knew she loved me."

Even couples who initially balk at the idea of writing admit, once they try, it gives them great freedom. They find they tend to be more honest when they write because there is no fear of being interrupted or prejudged.

Being able to write thoughts and feelings he found hard to express verbally "because the presenting couples made it so clear we should not judge each other's feelings" impressed Bob Warner. "I tended to play the role of the father figure and keep anything back that would make me seem less like the strong rock I thought I had to be. On the weekend I was sure what I wrote would be accepted by Dorothy, so it was much easier to explain and share my feelings."

Almost all communication in marriage is verbal conversation. The only exceptions are possibly anniversary and birthday cards or a letter when one is away. Or, occasionally, if there is something big on the mind and heart, it might be written out since it won't come out any other way.

"Clara had resorted to writing in the past when she had deep feelings—usually hurts—that she couldn't manage to express aloud," said Howie Davidson. From that experience, he had already learned "writing was a way to know Clara much better."

It seems fair to say, however, despite those who now and then write, that 95 per cent of all communication between husband and wife is verbal. The spoken word is good, of course. It is an absolutely essential form of communication between spouses. But it has definite disadvantages.

Husbands and wives—particularly those in good marriages who have talked together a lot—tend after a number of years to believe they know what the other person is going to say. They often finish the other's sentence, at least interiorly, and don't really listen to all that is actually being said. Cay Heiman recognized this tendency in herself. "I frequently jump ahead when John is speaking, prejudge and make assumptions before he is finished. My facial expressions apparently give away my reactions because we can have a fight before he has a thought completely verbalized."

Often we know the background or what the other person is looking for and want to short-cut, so we give the answer when the other has hardly begun. The person who starts the conversation is interrupted before getting a chance to finish and the interruptions go back and forth between them until they end up on a completely different topic. Hank Yudt said, "Before our weekend we interrupted each other constantly. There was seldom time to complete a thought or sentence. Usually I was the guilty one. I wasn't always that interested; I was too wrapped up in myself and constantly thinking of what I was going to say, so what Judy had to say was completely incidental."

We all fit Hank's description of himself at times. When someone else is speaking we really are not paying that much attention to what is being said because we are just waiting for our chance to speak. We already know what we are going to say. We listen with our answer running. For this reason the technique introduced on the weekend has become tremendously important to many couples, including Richie and Joan Fuerst. "I feel freer writing than I do speaking," Joan said. "My love flows freely from my pen while saying the words is sometimes difficult. Often in a conversation I lose track of what I wanted to say—or, if I'm interrupted, it's lost. Also to read what Richie has written, I have to hold still to read and hear his words, whereas when we talk I find my mind racing ahead or jumping to something else. It's calming to sit and soak up what he has written. The words have much more meaning when I hold them in my hand—see them with my eyes and try to feel them with my mind and heart."

Dick Holdren discovered: "I can keep rereading what I have written and that keeps the feelings alive. When you speak it's sometimes hard to be sure you said what you meant. At least when it's written you can alter it if it isn't right."

It is so true in talking back and forth that, even when we listen well, it is quite easy to lose the flow of what the other person is saying and even what we ourselves are saying. We don't really remember where we began. Quite often when we are discussing something important we don't speak our thoughts well because it means so much. We get all jumbled up in our own words, and it comes out garbled. The reverse occurs when one party has thought a subject through so well the other person can't cope with it on the first bounce.

"Sometimes when Bob says something he drops it like a bomb and then moves on," added Sheri Stritof. "It leaves me in a daze. When I have the opportunity to read what he's written, I have time to consider, reflect and respond rather than react to his feelings. There is time to remember not to ask why he had a feeling, to remember that feelings are neither right nor wrong. And there is a sense of Bob's loving me in his letters which helps me relax." "To my surprise, when I wrote I discovered I was able to express more of myself and stop overwhelming Jean with my words," Rita Gorremans said simply.

In speaking, the tone of voice in the first couple of words can set us off. We are convinced we know where this conversation is heading and we don't even give it a chance. Our own nonverbal reactions can well cause the other person to stop, back off or change the topic entirely. It might be a raised eyebrow, a frown, a stiff or trembling lip, or even tears. The other recognizes he is on touchy ground so he softens or modifies or changes the subject to something much safer. There is no possibility as we write of the other person's reaction turning us off or getting us to pull back from what we want to say. Because we are alone in facing the paper we can say what we really want to without fear.

For instance, there are things Chris Kenny couldn't look Don straight in the eye and say. "But," she said, "somehow when I'm writing everything I want to say pours out. It's like a break in a water pipe—it just keeps coming. Or like waves rolling into the shore—they keep coming. The words flow, and the excitement builds."

One of the real fears people have about writing is that they are not professional writers. They think that somebody who is an English major or has written a book has a big advantage. Actually, people who are professional writers find it harder to get into the weekend because they are concentrating on how they are saying things instead of on revealing themselves. They have to forget their skill and just become persons. The fact that a person does or does not find it easy to write really is quite irrelevant. No one has to be an English major—only a person.

It is not terribly important that we write anything awfully significant or tremendously deep. If we just start writing, our personhood will come out. Initially, of course, it is not always with the depth we would wish.

"At first," Anne Roney said, "I wrote in short, choppy phrases —sparking off ideas, thoughts and feelings. When I did write a feeling, I justified it in detail, telling *why* I felt a certain way rather than describing the feeling itself. As the weekend progressed I wrote more fully and more openly because Hugh accepted the choppy phrases and that encouraged me. The more deeply we became immersed in one another through our sharing, the freer I felt to share more."

Writing on the weekend was also difficult for Ralph Buisson. "I felt a constant pressure and was frustrated at first," he said. "The whole idea of feelings was so foreign that I didn't know where or how to begin. As the weekend progressed, however, I found it became easier to write; and for the first time I was able to communicate with Merce on a level I never dreamed possible."

We are distracted by something else that is going on, something on television we are watching together, a noise out in the street, the baby's cry. In conversation we can easily tune each other out. Perhaps we are afraid to stir up embers or to get pots boiling; we don't want to commit ourselves too much. We do really want to watch that show, and if we say the wrong thing, it is liable to lead to an hour's discussion. If something is churning within us, we pay only half-hearted attention to what the other person is saying, figuring if it is all that important it will stand out. We pick up the salient points, but we don't really give our full attention to each other most of the time. We hear the words, but we really don't respond; often we just give a nod or an "isn't that nice?"

Dick Kruszewski finds he "sometimes fades off, maybe thinking about what Mary Anne had just said, rather than really listening to what she is saying *now*."

One of the beautiful advantages of writing is that it affords equal time for the silent partner in a marriage. In many couples one is talkative and the other listens. Writing gives the listener a chance to be heard. This is a great experience for both of them. The voluble one frequently is that way because nothing is being said in return. He or she doesn't really want to do all the talking, but there doesn't seem to be any choice. The silent one gets a chance to organize what's going on inside of him or her and get it out.

One of the real difficulties in verbal communication is that husbands and wives tend to just start talking without thinking it through. Naturally, they tend to talk about the most obvious thing needing attention at any given moment, whether it be the income tax, or the child's homework or the bill to be paid. It is almost never the couple themselves. Many couples are like Carl and Sheila Henderson who say they are "very thing-oriented in conversations, discussing when to buy a new stove or refrigerator, how to cope with our son's teachers, etc. The things of our lives. We never really sit down and talk just about us, who we are, what our hopes, dreams, ambitions are."

It is the old squeaky wheel getting the grease routine. A definite decision to talk about us has to be made and through my experience in Marriage Encounter I've learned the "talking" is best accomplished through writing. If you were to put a husband or wife in a room by themselves and tell them they have some time to talk to one another, they would most probably sit there looking at each other, trying to decide what they should talk about. Almost automatically, conversation would veer to their in-laws, the job, vacation, pension plan, their savings or the like. They might even talk about Church, or God or prayer. But it is almost certainly guaranteed they are not going to talk about each other. Even if they do start there, they will be distracted by other things pressing in on them. All these disadvantages are overcome when we write. When we are writing we can't interrupt each other. We can, of course, still interrupt ourselves, but we are more aware we are doing it than when we're talking. Also, writing slows us down, helps us to see what we are actually saying and how we are saying it so we are not just blurting things out. If, perchance, it is coming out hard or harsh, we can see it and change it. A lot of times in verbal communication, because our feelings about the subject are so intense within us, we turn the other person off even though we don't intend to.

When writing we can finish sentences with no presumptions being made. There's a chance to put it all down. Even when distracted we can get it all down; it is easier to get back on track when writing, and force ourselves to pay better attention to what we are saying. It is also easier for the other person to "hear" the written word. He more easily gets the full picture. If it's garbled or disjointed, it is easier for him to fit it together. In reading we don't as easily lose the flow of what the other is saying.

One of the biggest advantages of writing was expressed by Father Tom Morrow: "It makes me listen to *myself*. When I know

I'm going to write, I have to take the time to listen and look at myself."

Sometimes we're surprised by what we discover through writing. "I thought I was in touch with my feelings, and I thought my wife was in touch with hers, but it wasn't until I started writing," Carbery O'Shea said, "that I realized how much I was really out of touch with myself, and with my own feelings. The more I wrote the more I realized the love I have for Mary."

One of the reasons many of us don't relate as well as we could is that we are not using our full resources. In the writing part of the dialogue technique, we can discover the richness within each of us. "She opened her heart and soul to me in her notebook—a little at a time—a little more each time," said Bob Stanton of his wife, "revealing to me the most beautiful person in the world. Needless to say, I fell in love with her all over again."

CHAPTER VII

The Love Letter

There is a pace and a tempo to Marriage Encounter; we go one step at a time with our couples. Friday night everyone is unwinding from their week. They are still half with us and half back home in the hurly-burly of job and house and children. By Saturday they begin to realize they are free. It is just the two of them. So we can go full stride.

When they first arrive we just ask them to write their feelings to each other. Now we suggest that they not merely get their feelings down on paper but that they do so in such a way as to describe them fully for their spouse for the sake of their relationship. It is not enough to just get the feelings out. It has to be in the context of their love for each other. We therefore ask them to write their feelings in the form of a love letter.

You know, I sit up there giving an Encounter, looking out at those twenty-five couples making the weekend. They are so good. They have so much love in them. By this time on the weekend I know them a little and I want so much for them to find their full richness.

It is very hard for some to write a love letter. I understand. I really do. It's been such a long time, or they're afraid of being laughed at or they don't think they'll be any good at it—1,001 reasons. My heart goes out to them. How much I want them to get over the barrier, just get them started. Once they start it will all happen. Sometimes I feel like a doctor with a patient who out of fear refuses to agree to a life-saving operation. It's so frustrating. In my mind, I'm all over that room trying to come up with something that will take the frown off that guy's face, soften the hard eyes of that girl, answer the question causing the puzzled look there. Oh, it's so important to just get the love coming through those pens. I try to think of every possible objection so I can answer it. I breathe a quick prayer that I might say the right thing. I try to tell them about love letters in just the right way. If I could only tell them how much their love for one another means to me. I care so much that sometimes I don't want them to know because it hurts when one or another couple refuses to try. I want to shout at them "Damnit, why should I care about your marriage if you don't." But I do.

This is often the first time a couple has written a love letter to each other. Sometimes they have been childhood sweethearts coming from the same neighborhood. Or, for others, so many years have passed since they have written to each other, the idea comes as a bit of a shock.

To Rich Meehan writing love letters sounded kind of Hollywoodish and mushy. "I thought they were putting me on, but I decided I would try. The first time I wrote it seemed awkward and forced. But when I finished and read it over, it seemed rather beautiful and I was kind of proud, and Pat seemed to appreciate it and that boosted my confidence. The second letter was easier to write. As I put my feelings in the book, I felt as if I was preparing a little gift for her."

The purpose of a Marriage Encounter is not self-development or even self-awareness. That may happen concomitantly, but the real focus of the weekend is building each couple's relationship and giving them the opportunity to become aware of their richness. If the end was self-revelation, we could just as well write our feelings for a counselor, a doctor, a priest or a trusted friend. But the point of writing is not just to discover myself. It is more than that. It is to allow my beloved to experience me, taste me, live in me. The focus is not on me; it is on us.

But despite the importance of the love letter concept to the dialogue, not many people receive the idea of writing love letters with great delight. Though they fade after a while, uneasiness and embarrassment are more common first reactions.

"The idea of receiving love letters from Ray seemed romantic but a little silly," said Beth Re. "But as the weekend progressed reading Ray's letter became a very serious, moving experience. His love letters were not gushy, but tender, honest and loving. As I read them I saw a Ray I never really knew before. Each letter opened doors which had been closed and locked."

Don Sautner said, "My first and strongest reaction was embarrassment. It sounded corny and forced, but I remember my reservations and inhibitions starting to gradually relax as I gradually accepted the love letter as a valid concept. But still, I was timid and hesitant about expressing *myself* in terms of a love letter even after I began to see the value of it. It seemed to open me up in a new and more total way to Jeanne, but even as I wanted the openness, I was unsure of myself and afraid of the outcome. I wrote because I wanted more for our relationship. As I look back it's doubtful either of us would have given or received as much if we had been writing in a form other than a love letter."

Donna Hand was embarrassed with the idea of love letters: "Because I wanted so much for Sam to feel my love, I was afraid I would put too much in it and would turn him off. At first, I wrote 'Dear Sam' and I signed 'I love you' but it was not deep at all. I really guarded myself. It was not until Sunday morning, when I had stopped thinking about myself, that I had the confidence to put everything into it."

Part of the reason for the hesitancy, of course, is that people equate love letters with gooey words. When we have something difficult to express, it may seem phony to call it a love letter. We are fearful we can't be honest, because we confuse love letters with just saying sweetie-pie things about one another. Yet, what actually happens is that the more loving the context, the freer we are to express ourselves.

"The deeper I got into writing in the form of a love letter, the more I got into my feelings," said Jack Atkinson. "I just went to pieces. I really began to pour myself out on the paper. Then I knew what was meant by 'love letter.' It was not a mushy-gushy thing. It was the real inside of me coming out and all the love I had to give just flowing."

In writing a love letter, there is always a temptation to hold back—put the emphasis on keeping things nice. But an essential quality to love is honesty since love is built on trust. Actually, when we think we're being nice for someone else's sake, it's more often for our own. So we have to be as real, as alive and as total as possible to our loved one in the words we share. Not to show how open we can be or how total or how lovable. What we are striving for is to make our loved one realize that he or she is loved very much—enough to be trusted with the full *me*."

It is very important that couples on the weekend realize style of writing is not important. Who, when they have received a gift of love, is going to quibble about style? Bob Stanton is probably typical of many men and women who come to the weekend. "It had been years since I had written anything more than a brief note or a business letter," he said. "My first few attempts were feeble, superficial. I was afraid of my wife's reaction. When I decided to trust her love for me, I began to open my heart and pour out my feelings and my love. She responded. Oh God, she responded to my love with more love. With her encouragement I began to discover and reveal who I really am, what I felt deep inside—and she loved me more than ever."

"I was used to writing to either make a point or get something off my chest," added Penny Christiansen. "But this was a love letter. A few times my self-confidence left me; but Richie's interest in what I wrote encouraged me to continue. I realized on that weekend that Rich is really sensitive. It was something I had never looked for or expected."

Ann Brennan testifies to a richness in the love letter. "I always knew that Pat was sensitive and tender, but not to that depth. However, it is all right there in the love letter. Who needs a will when you've got that?" What is being offered to any couple is an opportunity to share themselves through a love letter. It is a giving of self, and therefore the spouse is very much involved. It is not enough just to have self in mind while writing.

For Phil Dwyer, "the love letter is like burning a candle at both ends to be able to get more light and see better and then find out that the substance of the candle does not diminish with time but grows stronger. One end of the candle is me and I am discovering through dialogue I am becoming more aware of who I am, and the other end of the candle is Theresa. I honestly believe I am her mirror and her self-appreciation is in my control, especially in my love letters."

As we explain the love letter, we say if it is to be a true love letter, it has to reveal both parties. We suggest to those who have kept old love letters to each other, that they take them out and look them over again. Probably they are not going to be terribly impressed by what they had to say in their love letters to one another, but what is going to be on those pages is a tremendous desire for the other person, a tremendous yearning for him or her.

In a true love letter we may be writing about ourselves but we are writing about ourselves in relationship with our loved one, and therefore he or she is just as alive in our pages as we are. This is what we try to get across to our couples on the weekend as the focus of the love letter they are going to write. They are not to hold back their honest feelings, but they are to give them in terms of their awareness of their beloved and their earnest desire and urgency for him or her. We are trying to avoid having couples simply write a report of their feelings.

The basic thing to come out is *me*. Contained in the letter is an urgency to love our spouse and a desire for our spouse to love us. It isn't to let the partner know about us, but to let our partner experience us. The goal is not information; it is conformation. What dialogue offers is the opportunity to experience not the same *type* of feeling the beloved has, but the beloved's *actual* feeling of sadness or pain or happiness. The aim is not to give my partner an intellectual awareness of what is happening within me, but to give him or her the possibility of actually getting inside me to experience what I am experiencing in this feeling—a much higher goal and a much deeper experience. What we are striving for is a realization of the "two in one flesh" concept of sacred Scripture. It seeks to fulfill the commission given at the time of marriage to be "one in mind, one in heart, and one in affection."

Did you ever see an older couple who have been married a number of years, and notice that they even look alike physically? This is not an accident. Their life together has created the lines on their faces. If they have been a happy couple the wrinkles and smile lines are over their faces. If they have been an unhappy couple then the frown lines and the heaviness are also there. So it is not just the shrinkage of old age causing them to look alike; it is their life together. What we are trying to do as the result of the love letter is to create an interior life together.

In writing a love letter we have to be just as aware of the other person as we are of ourselves. We therefore have to build up a sense of his or her presence as we begin to write, not to distract us from the feelings going on inside us, but to share them in the most loving and meaningful way possible. Lovers have a language no one else understands. If someone other than a person's spouse can pick up a love letter and really understand it fully, it isn't a love letter. There are code words between lovers. A little incident can be typical of a whole lifetime together. Our words mean something special to the people we love and they probably will mean something different to everybody else.

Something that often prevents us from letting all the love within us out is our poor self-image. We doubt ourselves; we don't really think we are all that lovable. Many of us will admit to having felt the fear that Margie Roberts describes: "So often I was afraid to be totally open. I judged my own feelings and even in my love letters sometimes wrote how I thought I *should* feel instead of how I *did* feel. I wanted Howie to love the real me; I longed to be myself; but fear prevented me from being totally honest."

In a true love letter, our real hope is to let our loved one know how lovable and how worthy of our love he or she is. Some people don't see themselves as being loved no matter how hard their husband or wife may try to express love to them, because deep down they don't consider themselves to be worthwhile. All the earnestness on the part of the spouse to pour out love on them will not be accepted unless he or she decides to believe he *is* worthy. But we all need some help in believing in ourselves. That is why it is so important for our awareness of the goodness and the value of the person we love to come across in our letter. Love doesn't happen to us; incidentally, we make it happen.

"It takes a decision to believe in myself and in Mike's love for me just as I am," said Bonnie Russak. "In one letter I wrote to Mike about my concern that his conception of me was much better than what I really am. I told myself he didn't really have to be aware of my feelings for us to have a good marriage. But each decision to let Mike respond to me as I really am strengthened my faith in myself and in him and gave me a better appreciation of the two of us. I have never felt freer or more loved in my life."

The writing, of course, continues to center around feelings throughout the weekend. We strongly discourage confessions, any sort of search for past high crimes or misdemeanors or "pouring out" of grievances stored up over the years. Spewing out resentments and bad memories just doesn't enter into the weekend. That would only have a negative effect. It would either cause our partner to curl up inside or to flare back with a history of faults. We are not trying to destroy; we are trying to build.

When Judy Yudt came on the weekend with her husband, Hank, she had all sorts of things stored up. When she heard about the writing, she thought, "Now he'll have to listen." But then she discovered "there wasn't really that much to say. I was more interested in writing about us, in sharing my feelings," she said, "than about little things that had happened."

Marriage Encounter is a very powerful and deep experience, but it is not a harsh or rending one. It is not aimed at prodding us to show the "deep, dark side" of ourselves. But rather gives us an opportunity to show our tenderness and compassion—to expose the sunny side which we have kept hidden, because it seemed like a weakness, or because we feared it might allow others to take advantage of us. The love letter should reveal each of us as we are now. It is never intended to solve a problem, to change someone. It merely says, "*Here I am. Love me.*"

Absolutely vital to this whole business of dialogue is that a feeling can't be just identified; we are not after labels. Once we have discovered a feeling within ourselves—the deepest feeling we are aware of having—we reveal it and bring it to full bloom for our spouse. Sadness, tenderness, compassion, joy cannot be just named; for the personal dimension to appear, they have to be described.

The problem with merely identifying a feeling such as sadness is that the other person often says, "I know just how you feel," and they really believe they do. Maybe they even feel a bit sad now because we are sad. But unless I tell them more, they don't know how it feels for *me* to be sad right at this moment. When they say "I know how you feel" they mean "I know how I would feel if I were going through what you are." They are remembering their own feeling of sadness.

My feeling of sadness is not your feeling of sadness. When I am really down I have a tight feeling in my chest, my jaw is set with teeth clamped, I feel a burning on my skin, my eyes smart, my legs are heavy and my walk deliberate. Usually I'm very alert and lively but now I'm dull, uninterested and uninteresting. My mind is normally a swirl of ideas, plans and dreams. I frequently have sixteen balls in the air at the same time and I revel in it all. But when I'm sad I'm easily distracted and oppressed by anything that requires thought, while I focus in on the hurt I am experiencing. My whole mental process seems in slow motion. Usually when others talk to me I'm very much tuned in not only to what they say but to what they mean and where they're going. When I have the blues I have to ask them to repeat, and even then I don't follow very well. Sadness makes me want to hide. It's like a dark night without moon or stars—total blackness. My ears are filled with a roaring of discordant noises as if I were at an event picketed by two opposing groups. Sadness to me smells like a cocktail lounge the day after a busy evening filled with the odors of stale beer, cheap perfume, smoke and old cigar butts. It's like a cloying syrupy substance the taste of which just can't be washed away. The touch of my sadness is like fly paper —remove it from one finger and it sticks to another.

Feelings have to be described. Not an easy job, but worth the effort. "It's a joy to describe the happy feelings, and a relief to describe the frustrations of life, the depressions, the vexations," said Ann Ennis.

We do not describe feelings to win the other person's sympathy, to get our own way, to manipulate or make the other person change. We have to look intensely inside ourselves and find out exactly how we do feel. We must come to a full self-awareness by discovering what our most obvious feeling is, and then, what feelings surround that feeling.

How do we describe a feeling? The immediate reaction for most of us would be to explain our feelings—to justify them—or to give a source. What we actually ask couples to do on a Marriage Encounter is describe exactly the way a feeling is experienced—to describe it to the nth degree. To go into the depths of ourselves and describe what we find there. If two people feel just their own separate sadness there is no value to that. The aim is to feel what the other is experiencing, which in this case happens to be sadness. The thrust and the focus are to feel that person, to get inside his or her skin, and to be part of who he or she is. The result is a new closeness and an overwhelming exultation that both experience.

"Before the weekend we discussed surface feelings," said Penny Christiansen. "But we didn't explain or describe them. Two words we used often were 'happy' and 'sad'—but what kind of happy and sad? Richie would ask, 'Are you happy?' and I would say, 'Yes'; and I'd ask, 'Are you happy?' and he'd say, 'Yes,' and we'd leave it at that. It was intriguing to realize Richie didn't experience happiness or joy in the same way I did. In one of his love letters, Richie described the way he would feel if I were to die. We had never talked much about our own deaths. Of course, I assumed Richie would be sad if I died. But it was totally different to have him describe what life would be like for him without me. There was much more there than sadness. For instance, he told me he would feel confused, not knowing which way to turn. It started a lot of feelings stirring in me. I think that every area we touched on in that dialogue has made us much more determined to really appreciate each other and not take each other for granted."

In a way, the love letter is like a stopwatch. With a regular watch, that second hand goes around relentlessly, but with a stopwatch, we can click it and make it stop. We have it to look at permanently. The same is true when writing. We retain a specific feeling we are facing at the moment. When we talk about a feeling, we tend to settle for less. Much more is called for from us when we have actually to write about a feeling and describe it. Even then, because feelings are sometimes elusive, it can be difficult to keep our focus on a particular feeling. But at least, when we have written, we can see after the fact that we have wandered from our subject and alter our direction.

The effort we take to describe in full detail the precise feeling we are experiencing is part of making our revelation a love letter.

It shows how much we care that we would be so complete and so detailed. But we must always keep the other person in mind. It is not merely self-revelation. It is not just opening; it is reaching out to include the other person.

"Reading our love letters was like unwrapping gifts of love to each other as we shared our innermost feelings and found they revealed the lost world we once knew as lovers," said Buzz and Dee Buzzoni.

The old saying has it that the wife is always the last to know. I had an experience of that on a weekend. What she was the last to know had nothing to do with his outside activities. It was him she was the last one to know.

When the couple I am thinking of came in on Friday night, it was evident she was distraught. He was very solicitous about her, but she almost ignored him. On Saturday night he came to me and told me he didn't know how much longer he could stay. He wanted to leave the weekend because he felt if he stayed he would break down and he didn't think his wife could take that. He explained that she had never recovered from the death of their little girl. Although he was doing his best to be strong for her sake, the ache in his own heart for his little girl was getting worse and worse, and he was afraid his collapse would only increase his wife's grief. She depended on him and needed him to lean upon. "She just cries all the time; she misses our little daughter so and it's tearing me apart," he said. "I can't hold on much longer; how empty my life is since she died."

I tried to persuade him to share those feelings with his wife, but he was afraid she couldn't take it. Finally I took him to the chapel and asked him to just pour out his heart to her in the greatest love letter he ever wrote. About three hours later both of them burst into the room. Both their eyes were red from weeping, but the smiles on their faces held out promise. For those two years since the child's death she had felt all alone. She believed it mattered only to her. How bitterly she resented that he never showed anything. He hadn't even cried when their daughter died or at the funeral. In that love letter his true feelings came out. It meant so much to her to know that he cared. Now she could trust him with her heart, and he didn't have to pretend to be a rock for her any more. His love letter opened them out to one another.

CHAPTER VIII

Learning to Read

It's funny but right from the first Encounter I ever gave up to the present the word I use to close every presentation and send the couples and priests to their reflection and dialogue has been "enjoy." To me it is much more than a sign-off word, more than a signal that the presentation is over and it is time for us to begin writing. The word is very precious to me. It comes from a deep hope in me for each couple and priest on the weekend. It is a commission to them to rejoice in the fullness of who God has called them to be to each other. I look on "enjoy" as my word in the Encounter. It sums up what I am all about.

Yet often the reaction to me is similar to that expressed by Mariann Murphy: "Our first experience with Chuck was on our team training weekend. I don't think I have ever been as afraid of anyone as I was of Chuck. I don't think I experienced apprehension to that degree with anyone else as I did with him. I sensed on that weekend that he could see right through me, that he had an unusual insight into people and what they were feeling. It was as if there was a zipper down the front of me that let him see right through me, as if he knew more of who we were than we knew ourselves. It frightened me that he should know so much about us. Really about us—who we were."

That's such a contrast, isn't it, enjoy and fear. I want so badly for couples to get inside each other. I'm all keyed up, using everything I've got. Every moment of every weekend for me is a time to persuade, cajole, plead with and encourage each couple to be open to one another. I really don't care if they listen to me, if they only listen to one another. It's all there—the closeness, the joy, the richness, the hopes that keep searching for fulfillment. If only they are present, truly present to one another, they will never be alone any more; and then they will enjoy.

St. Theresa, the Little Flower, was canonized by the Catholic Church because she did ordinary things in an extraordinary way. Kitty Kallen had a hit record a long time ago that drove the point home: "Little Things Mean a Lot." Football is known as a game of inches. It is this realization we try to impress on our couples on the weekend—every little detail of the dialogue technique has an importance all its own. Alone, by itself, each may seem insignificant, but if each is done with fullness it adds to the whole picture.

Each part of a Marriage Encounter leads us to be more personal with each other. We want couples to be more aware of themselves and to listen, really listen, to themselves and each other. Not just to words, but with a total sensitivity and responsiveness to each other. When we really listen we become aware of our infinite variety and depth. There is so much more to us than we ever dreamed.

One of the real purposes of the love letter is to put dynamite charges underneath our conviction of ordinariness and see the extraordinary. It is so easy in our everyday life to take each other for granted. We tend to pay attention only when there is a problem. Reading the love letter brings the miracle of understanding. It is not meant to be glanced over but experienced.

What brings couples together in the first place is that they noticed something special about the other person and started to date. What brought them to marriage was discovering how important they were to each other, how they valued each other, how they listened and cared. They were never shut off or tuned out when they were dating. What the other person said didn't have to be earth-shattering. Just the sound of the loved one's voice was enough. They could never share enough ideas; they never wanted to stop being together.

At that time, a couple was important, totally important, to each other. No matter what was said, it counted very much. On a Marriage Encounter we can recapture that joy, the exhilaration of being listened to again. We have a chance to express more of ourselves to each other, than we ever had before, to learn how much we care. How often do we say: "Will you please listen to me?" The dialogue offers a golden opportunity for us to listen, to be listened to, to accept and to be accepted.

If you've ever seen an O. J. Simpson run or a Walt Frazier steal the ball, it looks so natural. It's done so effortlessly. We don't see the years of tedious practice and effort-filled sweat that make them the stars they are. We believe they're just talented. Yes, they have talent, but it is a developed talent. They have paid a big price for it. They have paid attention, they have listened, they have trained every muscle to notice opportunities. Marriage Encounter is a training camp for love. Dialogue is the calisthenic to get our listening muscles toned up, at their peaks. We have to do every aspect of this exercise intensely to get the full benefit. The exercise itself is not important. It's that it builds us up and makes us more capable of truly listening.

On the weekend, the atmosphere helps couples gradually relax into greater responsiveness to each other. "Initially neither of us listened," said Dave and Eileen Murphy. "We were both more interested in each other's reaction to what had been written. By Saturday afternoon we were beginning to tune in to what the other was saying, and by Saturday night we were really listening with our whole bodies, not only our ears."

Part of learning to listen to each other is making the effort to shut out our surroundings and focus on our spouse. "We really tried to put aside the distractions of the other couples," said John Clark. "To be open to Barbara requires an intensive concentration on my part to listen, not just with my ears but with my whole body. It is very hard work to listen; it takes a lot of effort. Touching sometimes makes me feel a little uncomfortable, but I am very much aware of how it too is communication, and of how much I get from Barbara this way. There are things that I usually am not conscious of. For instance, when Barbara gets nervous and is holding my hand she starts to rub the skin on my thumb with her thumb. It is a very irritating sensation. I remember once clamping my hand over her thumb till she stopped doing it. Then I realized that Barbara was saying she is nervous. This little habit tells me something about her."

At the end of the writing time the couples are notified it is time for them to get together in the privacy of their rooms to share their love letters with one another. This time of movement seems very prosaic, so it is easy enough to yield to the temptation to daydream on the way in the minute or two that it takes to reach one's room. We point out to the partners who are moving that their spouse is still in the room writing, still absorbed in their love for them. Therefore, it is not really fair to be distracted from their spouse even during this short period of time. This transition time should be used to build up yearning and desire to read the beloved's love letter and to have him or her read yours. On the weekend there is no time out from love.

In the exchange of our notebooks, we are trying to open up to one another. It is very hard to listen, to be disposed to read uncritically what the other is going to reveal. Yet, even though they may feel awkward at first, couples find an excitement building as the weekend progresses.

Pat Brewster "could not wait to get to the dialogue. I felt something happen between us," she said. "We were communicating on a level we had never experienced before. We really could not wait to get to the room to read our notebooks. There were always surprises. Something was happening between us and I wanted it to continue."

"I only wish we could have that beautiful mood of predisposal every single day, as we had toward every single dialogue on that weekend," Betty Ann Connolly said. "As soon as that bell rang I couldn't get to the room fast enough. It was as if each exchange and dialogue period was another petal being added to a flower, and I could hardly wait to see what it would be like."

Julia Gee was so anxious to read Ken's letters that she "felt like running through the halls to get back to the room. Everyone seemed to walk so slowly," she complained. "Why did they? I wanted to call 'fire' so that they would get out of the way. *But* I had to control myself and act like the others."

It is amazing on a Marriage Encounter weekend to see the difference in the couples as they begin to listen to each other in depth. This is caused not by what they find in Marriage Encounter but by what they discover in each other.

Being totally aware of the other person is what it is all about. It begins with letting the other person be truly present to me in his or her notebook—giving my full attention to the reading.

The love letter is going to be wasted if it does not get us inside each other. Consequently, it is not just writing that is important, but also, while reading, being totally and fully absorbed in drawing the person off the page. In a true love letter, it is my beloved on the page. There I want to discover the person I love so tenderly and who loves me so much. The reading period is a special time, not a mechanical step to hurry over so we can get to the verbal dialogue.

Each step in the whole dialogue process leads to the next. If I am rushed or casual in reading, then the dialogue itself will fall flat. Reading my beloved's love letter to me should lead me to be tremendously conscious of him or her. But for this to happen I must fully concentrate on getting to the person behind the words. I have to put all the faculties at my command to work at absorbing my beloved.

This concentration would be impossible to achieve without the writing. Speaking is just too quickly there and gone. We have to draw the other person up off the page.

Dolores Genovese said, "Because I have quick, spontaneous reactions, often I respond to the words instead of to the person speaking. Reading gives me the chance to find the person behind the words. Reading also gives me the time to decide if my reaction is really to Lenny or if it is set by the mood I am in at that particular moment."

Bruce Turley found, "When someone is speaking to me my mind tends to want to answer what I hear before I've heard all that's being said." His wife, Doris, added: "When I read something and don't understand right away—it's still there the way it was meant to be said and I can reread to try again to comprehend. It doesn't go away. When Bruce talks, a look on my face might cause him to alter or temper his words and not really say what he wants to say to me."

All our training in reading teaches us to gather information and retain it. For many of us the only reading we pay close attention to in our normal life is a contract, a lease, a mortgage, a pension plan. We train ourselves to be most attentive to those because the consequences can be far-reaching. In almost everything else we read with half an eye. We merely want to get the gist of what we read. The details we can fill in afterward should we miss any.

It is a serious thing, this reading. We read twice; once for the head, once for the heart. First to find out what we thought was said, and then to find out what actually was said.

The purpose of reading for dialogue is not to find out *about* the other person but to be touched by him or her in the deepest sense of the term. It is to allow the other person inside me, not to have him look at me but to look into me. We ask couples to pay full and close attention to the love letter, not only with their minds but also with their hearts. We ask them not to read it just for the *what* but most especially for the *who*. To read between the lines to get into the person who has written this and not just read over what has been written.

"Ralph's writing helped me to concentrate on what he was saying and who he was then," said Merce Buisson. "I was not concerned with defending my views. I felt trusted and I understood him better than ever, because his writing was so straightforward and it seemed to say more than he ever did verbally. Or maybe this time I was really listening to him," she conceded.

Reading with great seriousness and great intensity and great attention really to discover the full richness in that letter is the chance—a chance many never have—really, to listen to the heart and soul of the beloved. It is a truly great experience to learn how to accept who my spouse is. This does not just happen. No matter how sincere and serious we are with the love letter, really being able to read it with a full awareness and acceptance doesn't happen automatically. All too often in listening as we read we see what we want to see. We add a "but" or an "and" to what is there instead of really taking her as she is.

As we read we have to concentrate on openness, reaching out to experience the true, beautiful, wonderful person we married. The love letter is not to discover the person that I think is there or the person I would like to find there, but to find the person *actually* there, the person of my beloved without distortion. Total openness toward the person I love is the essential starting point. Without an attitude of gentle acceptance or, to put it more strongly, a definite prejudice *toward* my beloved and her love for me, what she says will seem ordinary.

Hank Yudt thought, "The weekend was going to be a great chance to find out about Judy. I pictured the weekend as being for Judy. Through the writing, I discovered her, through being forced to read and forced to listen, I found out what was going on inside her, which was very unique. It was the wonder of discovering her."

We ask our couples to remember that those notebooks are love letters. We ask them to exchange their love letters with signs of affection—with gentle love and a special mark of affection as with a personal gift. We hope to build up between them a yearning to read each other's love letters, to create an atmosphere of reverence in the exchange. A mood just doesn't happen, it is built.

Something fascinating is the embarrassment that couples experience when they come to each other with a notebook in their hand. They feel very awkward and don't know quite what to do. Naturally, whenever any of us are ill at ease we tend to be very casual to hide our embarrassment.

"I found it awkward and waited for Steve to make the first move. I thought these signs of affection should come naturally and no one should suggest to us to do this," was the response of Diane Del Rey.

Fred Emry said, "When Connie first read my love letters it was as though I had asked her the question 'Would she accept me?' That is a time of feeling very vulnerable like offering someone a gift which means a lot to you, and the other person has an opportunity to accept or reject it in varying degrees. That's vulnerability."

As the weekend progresses, couples begin to understand the reason for affectionate exchange. In fact, it becomes quite natural for them. Curt and Barbara Miles said, "Exchanging with affection made us feel like young kids, sort of like first loves. We were eager excited, awkward, uncertain."

Cindy and Bill McCafferty added, "On our first night we looked upon it as a formality and it seemed contrived and unnecessary. However, as we read each other's letters, and discovered the delight that sharing our innermost feelings brought to each other, a kiss or a hug became more natural. The meaning of exchanging notebooks with affection became a gesture of love, like giving the other a special and unexpected gift."

As we mentioned, growth in using dialogue comes from a steady pull during the course of the weekend. Friday night we deal with externals. Saturday morning we get raw feelings on paper. Later we escalate to love letters. In discussing feelings, we ask the couples please not to quarrel with each other's feelings, to remember that feelings are neither right nor wrong, to take the person just as he or she is. In asking them not to try to change the other, not to hope to give the other what you think is a better feeling, we point out how easy it is to reject one another's feelings.

"I still have a tendency to want Fran to always feel 'good,' and when her feelings are negative, to try to get her out of that condition or situation by suggesting 'there's no reason to feel that way,'" stated Skip DeBlasio.

Rejection isn't necessarily harsh. We don't have to say, "That is a stupid feeling," "How can any mature woman in the twentieth century feel as you feel?" It could be as seemingly innocent as "Gosh, dear, I never knew you felt this way, and it is so good of you to let me know how you do feel; now that I know you feel this way I won't do this any more." Or "Gee, darling, to know you feel that way is a great gift to me. And that is just an awful feeling. What can I do to help?" In both cases what is being said is that the feeling is a bad one. Because I love you, I don't want you to feel that way. I will do anything to take it away from you. The expression of it is nice, tender and gentle, but at root it's saying you shouldn't feel that way, get rid of it.

In the beginning of the weekend we merely ask our couples not to quarrel with each other's feelings, not try to change them. Then as we go along deeper into the Encounter experience we seek a much greater openness—a willingness to be so responsive that we are drawn through reading the love letter toward the feeling the beloved is experiencing not because the feeling is so attractive in itself but because one's spouse is.

It's really making an act of faith in our partner, faith that he cares enough about me to really listen and to exert himself in order to experience what I am experiencing. It is a faith in him that he even wants to know me better, that he is not just so tied up in his own concerns and in his own satisfaction that he would not be willing to work that hard and that lovingly.

CHAPTER IX

The Art of Communication

A frequent objection people have to going on a weekend is "Well, look, we are married. We know each other." Marriage Encounter is one of the most beautiful and enjoyable ways to find out how wrong this assumption is.

"What was so great about the weekend was that I found my true wife," said Carl Lucidi. "I thought I knew her—her ideas and her ways—but I really did not. What she shared in the dialogue—what she noticed in me—totally wiped me out."

Dialogue with her husband for Sandy Schulteis "was like being blind since birth and on the weekend having surgery performed. With each dialogue bandages were removed," she said, "so I could see Ollie more clearly as the truly beautiful man he is."

Dialogue seemed so "basic and simple" to Rich Fuerst, "I couldn't believe that it would materially change our relationship. Then with each successive attempt I began to realize just how little we were really communicating with each other and how much more there was to Joanie than I had known."

The dialogue is precious to the teams. It has been a magnificent technique and help in developing their own relationships. In their hearts there is an urgency to pass it on to every couple on their weekend. They have a deep sense of responsibility to be as full as they possibly can, to hold nothing back so that no one will be deprived of an opportunity to experience dialogue in as complete a way as possible on the weekend. Teams sense that a wonderful trust has been placed in them by the couples who have come to make the weekend. They do not want to let them down in any way.

Dialogue is a reminder of what marriage is all about—*us*. Marriage is not an institution, not a bastion of society. It is not a baby carriage, a service organization or social security for a woman and comfort and convenience for a man. It is the fullest, richest, most wonderful, most imaginative, most exhilarating possibility that life has to offer, *us* in relationship with one another.

The aim of dialogue is not to do better by each other or to settle differences, or even to learn more about the other person. Its goal is unity: to be one in heart. We may not achieve such a lofty aim with one dialogue, perhaps not with many. But each time we dare to trust each other with the most intimate part of us, our feelings, and hope actually to experience within ourselves what our partner is experiencing at that moment, we come closer to oneness—that is the pinnacle of love.

Were Marriage Encounter to stop with self-discovery, we would miss the point. Even writing love letters and stopping there would fall short. The whole process involved in dialogue is awareness of relationship. Everything in the Marriage Encounter —the presentation by the teams, the atmosphere on the weekend, the writing, the reading and the listening is to lead up to the couple's moments together.

After reading the love letters—twice for fuller understanding —the couple concentrates on one feeling to focus on and actually experience. It doesn't make a particle of difference whether the husband's or the wife's feeling is the subject of the verbal dialogue. If he experiences her feeling or she experiences his, both profit immeasurably. Regardless of whose feeling is the focus, it is an exhilarating, overwhelming experience for both. It is the conformation we have been talking about: a chance to taste, to bite into, to get a real sense of the experience the beloved is going through at this instant.

What we are aiming at through dialogue is a quantum leap. We are not talking about enjoying from outside the feelings of the spouse. What we seek is actually to taste the feeling. To have the seedling of that feeling planted inside me where it can grow. To really be experiencing what the other person is experiencing at this time in the same way. That is what the whole dialogue technique is all about.

After reading the love letter for the second time, we ask the other person to tell us more about what he or she is feeling. To describe it fully and carefully. Both partners have to be active participants in that description, feeding the other person with better ways to describe the feeling; the whole burden can't be left on one partner to make that feeling come alive. We describe back the feeling the way it is coming across, asking is this correct, is that what you are experiencing, and is this the way you are experiencing it? In a way it has to be like the police artist. The police artist goes to the witness and says, "O.K., describe the man who robbed you." So the witness gives a description and he draws a few lines on a paper, and he holds it out to the witness and says, "Now is this the man?" And the witness says, "Well, no, his ears are a little bit lower and his jaw more prominent." So the artist sketches again and he holds it out and he says, "All right, now is this the way he looked?" "Well," the witness adds, "he has a cleft in his chin and there was a mark on his left cheek." So the artist puts those in and says, "O.K., now is this the way the guy looked?" "Well, his hairline was more receded and his nose was slightly crooked." So the artist then makes those changes, and he says, "Now is this the way he looks?" and the witness says, "Yeah, that's it!" That is what we do in the dialogue. We go back and forth describing one feeling in more and more detail for the sake of the other person so that he can experience it and take it on too. Of course that won't happen every time we dialogue. Nor do we expect it to, but just the fact that we care enough to make the effort brings so much closeness and so much greater awareness.

Of course this process of describing feelings doesn't seem natural at first. As with any new experience, we feel uncertain and self-conscious. "Dialoguing in the beginning was very uncomfortable, an awkward experience," said Ralph Buisson. "It was like walking in an unfamiliar house in the dark. You stumble around but keep on going until finally you begin to see. But the more we tried it, the closer we became. It opened the door."

Joe Marchese said, "Initially I was very uncomfortable with the dialogue. The idea of reading about Nancy's feelings and talking about them scared me. I did not know how to handle or deal with it. Fortunately, we kept with it for the weekend as it brought us closer together and I began to see I did not have anything to be afraid of."

During the dialogue we never ask "Why do you feel that way?" for cause is irrelevant. We ask questions such as "Tell me more about the feeling," or "Is this the way you feel?" or "Have I ever described a feeling to you like the one you are experiencing now?" We offer no reasons, only descriptions of what is so close to the core of us. . . . Nor do we assign blame. I do not expect you to be sorry for an action or comment that might have aroused a feeling in me. I simply want you to experience a part of me. I am sharing this feeling because I want you inside of me. Your feeling is important because I want a taste of you.

Lovers really talk this way. They talk about getting inside of one another or being one with each other. They say, "You are my alter ego. There is no me without you." Bear hugs and love bites and just drinking each other in with their eyes—all these are ways of expressing the yearning in the heart of the true lover to make his beloved part of his life and to immerse himself in the life of his beloved.

Most of us have thought of a thousand excuses for holding back from sharing ourselves with each other. "She is such a good woman she could not really cope with what is going on inside of me." Or, "If I tell her this, she will feel let down, she will not be able to rely on my strength any more." Or, "This feeling of mine would worry him too much. He will always be trying to make me feel better." Being able to share a feeling without embarrassment or hope for change or desire for self-improvement creates a peaceful atmosphere.

Dialogue, for Cay Heiman, brought "relief, freedom and great joy. I had always had trouble sharing my innermost feelings with John. I feared his judgment. It was an overwhelming joy to be able to give him the fullness of me. I couldn't write fast enough. The hope for the future was like being told that a diagnosis of terminal cancer had been an error and I was in perfect health."

There are some experiences where the fringe benefits are more rewarding than the direct benefits of other experiences. Dialogue is like that. The aim of dialogue of course is the experience of the other person and the coupleness that results. However one of the fringe benefits is that each dialogue gives more of an opportunity to see myself most accurately and meaningfully in the eyes of my beloved. Because the truth of the matter is, my spouse is much more aware of my goodness than I am.

"I discovered some pieces of myself, but I didn't find a very nice and perfect self," said Ging Le Jour. "There were lots of disappointment for me and I was afraid to give all that to Jacques. But I decided to be true and every time I pulled out a bit of the real me, often negative in my eyes, I realized Jacques accepted me and, even more, that he loved me more than ever. It was like receiving oxygen. I felt as if I were coming up from a narrow, dark pit. Sun, light and warmth came from Jacques' knowing me as I really was. I started to feel free to be myself."

Most of us have a very low image of ourselves. We may have a great deal of confidence in our capabilities, and our influence on others or what we can accomplish, but when we look at just ourselves without our skills and accomplishments, we really don't think that we are all that much. We look at ourselves as ordinary, as nothing special, although that is a completely false picture. Actually each of us is special; each of us is very lovable.

The person who has the best and the most intimate and the most aware knowledge of you as a person is your spouse. He or she is much more conscious of how special you are and how lovable you are than you could ever possibly be. What you have to do is allow his or her opinion of you to become your opinion of yourself; look at yourself with your partner's eyes, see yourself reflected through your spouse.

The weekend allowed Joe Cinege to see himself in a clearer focus: "Prior to the weekend I seemed vague and out of focus like a fuzzy photo. But dialogue allowed me to perceive myself in a new light. It was like putting on glasses for the first time or focusing a movie projector so I could finally see myself. I saw Cindy as a beautiful flower. She was so much more lovable to me after the dialogue, primarily because I was overwhelmed with the effort she gave to understanding me."

Part of the struggle for Tom Healy was a fear of losing control. "It was O.K. for Tia to take on my feelings," he said. "She was my wife, belonged to me. But the concept of me taking on *her* feelings scared me. I was afraid I would not have control and that taking on her feelings would modify me in some way and I would not be myself any more. I would become someone different. What happened of course is that I did open up and I did experience some of Tia's feelings. Every so often and to one degree or another that has been happening since the weekend, and I am still me and I still have my feelings. But there is a whole new dimension added on, a whole new understanding and awareness, and it is not restrictive. It is an expanding experience that is enabling me to be, for us to be and to do things and to love in the way that would never be possible otherwise."

Initially, many people share Tom's fear of losing their personhood, of getting lost, swallowed up by the partner. When the dialogue is explained that doesn't happen. There is no giving up; there is no giving in; there is simply giving. No other experience is like it in the world. A person costs something—I give up either something I have or the money it cost to buy it. There is no resentment or sense of deprivation in giving you that present, but I *have* given up something in order to get you that gift. In dialogue it doesn't work that way. If I give you my feeling and you actually take it on, I don't have any the less of the feeling. I still feel my feeling to the same degree I always did. If you take on my feeling, you have lost nothing. It is a unique experience of human communication. Similarly, in a discussion, if we have different positions either I have to give up my position or you have to give up yours, or we both have to come together somewhere in the middle in order to reach agreement. That never happens in the dialogue. We can have totally diverse feelings. Perhaps you are very, very sad, and I am very, very joyful. Now sadness is not worse than joy, nor is joy necessarily the feeling that both of you should aim at trying to experience. It really doesn't make any difference whether I try to take on your sadness or you try to take on my joy. Either way, if we succeed there is going to be ecstasy.

"What sticks in my mind about the dialogue on the weekend is reading the love letters and being filled with each other," Liz McCarthy remembers. "The thought of looking at Dennis, seeing his face, having him touch my face, doing things that we hadn't done since dating because now we had sex and had neglected all those little extras. As a matter of fact, we didn't make love during the whole weekend because we didn't have to, the extras were fun for a change. It was just good. It was like bathing for the first time in the love Den has for me. I glimpsed it in the past, knew it was there, loved him—but the joy of soaking in love—of feeling it like sun on the beach in August was so different, so total, I found myself crying the whole weekend long from joy, although I never cried in my life as an adult before."

Mike Kauer said, "On Saturday night we seemed like high school kids. We would dialogue, look at each other and kind of giggle. It brought joy right out of our mouths. It just could not be controlled. It just seemed like a natural thing to do."

Touching is a very important aspect of communication. We use the word "touch" to show that someone really got to me, really had an effect on me. We say "He touched me with his story" or "I was really touched when I saw her." All we're saying is that it's more than just an intellectual comprehension when moments like this occur. There is a real personal awareness. Such occurrences are not necessarily connected with physical contact. However, without a doubt, physical contact is an important way of being personal with another person. Communication can be nonverbal as well as verbal. As a matter of fact, when someone really does experience another person, there is an instinct within us to reach out, physically as well as interiorly. In the couple relationship, touching is very important—holding hands, a gentle touch, a soft caress, a hug—showing the other person that we really care. It makes it easier to say things that are difficult. Touch releases our tongue, opens our ears and gentles our hearts.

According to Tom Healy, on hearing about nonverbal communication, "The very first thing I thought of was something with sexual overtones. I said, 'Aha. Now we can get a little petting into this weekend.' That was when I was still fighting the feelings, still pushing to get some of my way into our relationship. But the thing that really caught me, the first inkling of what they really meant as far as the communication aspects of touching, was that when I really was trying to share deep things, things that I was a little bit nervous sharing, my eyes would wander off. Instead of looking at Tia, they would go look out the window or at the ceiling or at the floor. When I started to try to justify or try to prove the feeling, instead of trying to hold hands, I would pull my hand away and wave it around like when I am arguing or something. I did not realize it. I always thought the Italians talk with their hands. The Irish never did. I never realized how much this Irishman talks with his hands. I began to notice, and it became a signal to me that I was either holding back or trying to justify whenever my hands were trying to pull away from Tia. My eyes would start to look at someplace else and not to focus on her. When I discovered that in myself I began to notice it in Tia too. I began looking at her and I started to pick up other signs of feelings like nervousness, tenseness, tenderness by trying to concentrate with my eyes and watching her face. Along with that came the observation of the rest of the face: the smile, the frown, the tenseness and the forehead, and the relaxful face. On the Encounter I came to a kind of deepening awareness but it was gradual."

Part of listening of course is touching. That is what alerts us to the fullness of the other person. Through the expression on the face, the tone of the voice, the way the eyes move, the trembling in the hand, the stiffness of the muscles, we pick up things about each other.

We can't dialogue across the room. If one of us sits in the chair and the other lies on the bed, what we do is chat. We aren't going to dialogue. For true dialogue we have to be close enough to experience each other as much as possible. So much can be learned from the coldness of the hand, the goose bumps on the arm, the trembling fingers, the sweat on the palms, knotted muscles in the back. It is one thing to see your tears running down your cheeks, it is another to feel your tears running down my cheeks and still a third to feel *our* tears running down *our* cheeks. The importance of touching in experiencing the fullness of the other person is one of the things a couple learns when they first meet. They are always in physical contact, holding hands, walking arm in arm. We are creatures of flesh and blood, we are not just creatures of soul. We have to use every means at our disposal to communicate.

Touching each other with our eyes is a most important part of dialogue. This truly makes us present to one another. So often we are busy about many things—putting away the dishes, reading the newspaper, watching TV, driving the car—that we don't look at one another as we talk. Even when we are facing one another, how often do we look into each other's eyes. Looking into each other's eyes takes the emphasis off the *what* and concentrates us on the *who*. The eyes are the windows of the soul. We have to speak not only with our tongues but with our eyes. We have to draw the other side, not only through our ears but also through our eyes. Looking deep inside this way is true intimacy.

"Wow!" exclaimed Don Sautner, "I really cringed at eye-to-eye contact. It didn't scare me so much as it completely turned me off as a cornball idea. I did it simply because I was determined to go along with every part of the weekend, and it made me realize how difficult it is to look into Jeanne's eyes when I want to conceal part of myself. But even as the eye contact made us each more vulnerable, it brought gentler responses and a kind of timid newness."

"That was the crunch," said Phil Dwyer. "I knew that we weren't into a staring contest, which I could probably win, but an honest opening up to allow Theresa to see who I was and who she was. My first reaction was 'no way'—that's too much too fast."

The dialogue itself is an act of faith in us. It is saying we are worth the effort. We don't have to make the right decisions. We don't have to do the right thing, we don't have to live up to the standards that have been held up to us as husband and wife. All we have to do is to be absorbed in one another, be aware of one another, be sensitive to one another, be responsive to one another. Once we are on the way and have made a commitment to continue in that direction, everything else fits into place. The truth of the matter is that the happiest years of our lives together were when we didn't have a sou. Probably we didn't have the money to pay the bills and we didn't have the gorgeous furniture and all the accouterments around the house we now have. We may not have had all these things, but we had the whole world because we had each other. Dialogue brings back hope, a chance to recover what we lost of each other.

Dialogue is a time when we want to get so close to each other's soul that we long to be completely one, a time filled with yearning to be more. It is a special time when we are most actively working at our goal of unity as a couple.

Dialogue for Joan Fuerst was "intense and personal." She

called it "offering yourself as a gift to another human being and accepting them in return. I don't know," she added. "There's something almost holy about this dialogue. I'm aware of God's stake in this. A good conversation is more a sharing of ideas. It gives me a sense of satisfaction and pleasure; but the 'holy' feeling isn't there."

Dialogue unites us, guides us to the highest possible achievement for a couple. "Eye has not seen nor has ear heard what God has prepared for those who love Him," said St. Paul in describing heaven. We can also say, "Eye has not seen, nor has ear heard what God has prepared for those who love one another. Truly such an experience between husband and wife is a bit of heaven. It makes this earth a paradise."

In describing the intimacy the weekend brought them, Dom Esposito said, "I went up to the room and said, 'You know, Josy, something's happening. I can't explain what it is.' We really got into each other, down deep. It's almost unbelievable how we would seem to become one. It seemed like I was becoming a new person."

"I wanted everything the weekend was offering us—the whole package," said Margie Samson. "Something happened inside me. Something rich and warm and beautiful; and I learned how important Stan was to me and how important our Father was to me and to us. Thinking about it now really fills me with excitement and joy for what I have in Stan and our love."

CHAPTER X

The Continuing Dialogue

For five years I lived at Gonzaga Retreat House for Youth and gave retreats to over six thousand seniors in high school. Sometimes between retreats when no kids were there I would walk the corridors thinking of my kids and what was happening to them. They meant a great deal to me. Many of them were so good, kids with high ideals and great dreams. The retreat experience was a powerful one for them. A lot came back to the Church, some reconciled with their families, others began to hope again. They walked out of that retreat house ten feet tall. But I knew that, for all but a handful, a couple of weeks or a couple of months later they would have lost most of it. It had been a great weekend for them but no matter how strong a retreat they had had they ended up pretty much where they started. Gosh, it hurt. One night I remember hearing about a kid who had had a wonderful retreat the previous year flunking out of school and going on the bum. That was it! I resolved if I ever got into anything else, it would have to have a built-in follow-up program. I know myself; I'm an all-out kind of guy. Whenever I get into something I go all the way and it just hurts too much if it doesn't last.

I was determined to find something more durable, more lasting, than just a terrific weekend. So, the daily dialogue, or the 10/10 as we call it, is what makes Marriage Encounter for me. It would just rip me apart on Sunday afternoons to see those couples so close and know it wasn't going to last. The last thing in the world we want is to give couples a pleasant interlude, a flash of sun, a weekend high. Our whole yearning for our couples and priests is that they take the weekend home with them. We're not providing a honeymoon, but pointing the way to a life of love.

Mario Menelly shared his views of the daily dialogue, "Without it," he said, "it would have been just another weekend, a great experience, but one we probably would have just forgotten about. There would have been nothing to keep us going. Without a daily commitment we wouldn't talk about the things we dialogue about." To Chris Suriano, Marriage Encounter "clicked because it was a continuous situation, and you take it home with you. You don't have to reproduce the weekend."

The weekend experience is simple enough. Couples come on Friday night ready to follow the instructions of the weekend. As they zero in on feelings, write and dialogue, their focus centers more and more on each other. Through their concentration in dialogue, they begin to discover the wonder and the mystery of their persons. The practice of dialogue on a daily basis is like planting the seeds of beautiful flowers that bloom, then fall to seed only to grow and bloom again, yet more lovely, yet more full.

Just to realize how lovable each of us is, that is a miracle in itself, and not one to be taken lightly. "You know," said Jo Rasmussen, "when I think about Charlie caring enough about me just to write me a love letter every day, I do begin to believe in myself—in Charlie's and Our Father's love for me."

To many people, the relationship of a dialoguing couple resembles that of newlyweds even though they may have been married for a long time. In our society this is a surprise because we are taught by example, if not by word, from the time we are little children to expect the luster and glow of romance to wear off. Even couples who are just dating are told to "enjoy it while it lasts." After all, they are reminded, they will have to get serious, settle down and assume responsibilities. So even though we might hope the glow would last, we don't really expect it to. When the focus begins to shift from each other to the activities of everyday life, the couple in love resign themselves to being ordinary people, not all that different from anyone else. We see it as proof of what we have learned: romance is infatuation; once the feeling goes, as it inevitably will, life goes on without it. The tragedy of the normal marriage is not the horror of divorce or separation or the major marital sins of adultery and cruelty but the willingness to settle down into a comfortable pattern of getting along with one another at a high level of accommodation. We believe this is the best we can hope to achieve. Implicit in this attitude is the old view that love is a feeling—variable, fickle and elusive—but we have to put our eggs in a more solid basket.

When a couple first meets and loves they have such dreams. Those dreams center particularly around their love for each other, their hopes and plans for their future together. Later they realize one of their greatest frustrations and sadnesses in life is that their early dreams now seem to be among the "might have beens" in this life. They have yellowed along with the wedding dress.

Marriage Encounter rekindles the possibilities they once held so dear to their hearts. It brings back the realization that they are special to one another and because of that, they are special to the whole world which surrounds them. It makes their love once again the most significant love in the world. Prior to Marriage Encounter had a couple gone on a quiz show where they were asked to name the three greatest love affairs in the history of the world, the answer might have been Antony and Cleopatra, Tristan and Isolde, and Romeo and Juliet. Now the answer loud and clear is "us," as it should be.

On the weekend we see how our decision to love grows into the feelings of love as dialogue brings us closer. We watch unity, oneness and an exhilarating closeness replace the old contentment. The couple will never be as they were before; the memory of the weekend leads to a heightened sensitivity and tenderness toward each other. But the real bonus is that it never has to end. Each time we dialogue, the grayness of our previous life dies a little more. The fullest gift of the Marriage Encounter is that it is theirs forever. It is a technique not for a weekend, but for a life-time.

"Daily dialogue is like food to me," said Father Jack Murphy. "Each day, even if I eat the same food, there is a different taste, a different flavor. Daily dialogue allows me, urges me, to try out different ways of tasting the same food [feeling]. It encourages me to eat more slowly, to savor each drop of wine, each morsel of lobster, each spoonful of creamy pudding. If I prepare the food [love letter] sloppily, hastily or without sufficient care, I get heartburn or indigestion. I eat quickly, try to get the meal over, run away. When I really put my whole heart and mind into the preparation I am never disappointed, never distracted, allow others to taste, enjoy and swallow without always looking for their reaction or approval. I know the food is good. I know I've put everything into it and I can enjoy more completely what others offer me. I am not always looking within to see if I've done my best cooking. I know that each day is new and wonder-ful and filled with new discovery."

As it turned out, I didn't have to worry about couples losing what they had gained; they were also concerned about losing it. There is a breath-holding on Sunday afternoon of a weekend. Couples look at each other with joyful fulfillment yet there is a touch of regret almost. They don't want to go home. They are afraid their closeness might slip away from them, and that they don't want. As Roz Brown explained it: "My one fear was that this would be like all my diets or my New Year's resolutions. Would the dialogue peter out like those? At least I was not alone in my resolution this time."

Cindy Cinege expressed a similar worry. "I was afraid of complacency settling in," she said.

Every human being is a mystery. We never know a mystery, but slowly it is revealed to us. Behind the shadows we discover the reality. On the weekend we look at the greatest mystery itself —the mystery of love. There is no such thing as a born lover. Love does not just happen; it is created through decisions we make, the give and take of day-to-day relationships and by reflection, listening and knowing ourselves, our strengths and our weaknesses. Love grows when we are being vulnerable, risking ourselves, dying to selfishness and giving ourselves over to the grace of love and the Father who is the source of all love. In love, we submit ourselves to one another so as to see into the depths of goodness in each of us—a goodness that knows no limit, for love is infinite. So the practice of couple love—love in the marital relationship—is really an uncovering of the mystery of God's goodness within us, and ultimately the very person of God Himself.

The practice of love requires a discipline. Not the discipline of law or rule, but that of steady practice. The word "discipline" comes from "disciple," which originally meant to submit oneself to a master in order to learn and grow. Discipline does not come easily to us, for we all have a streak of independence and stubbornness. As Annette Cooper testifies, "I am sometimes reluctant to be disciplined. Yet I long for the growth in our relationship brought about by this daily effort."

Pam Dugas learned, "It's the best way to be with Jean. We have our duties every day, and more or less go through the daily routine. When we come to our dialogue it's like having your dessert after a good meal. It's exciting—I can't think of another word but that, to describe it. It's our chance to be close and open and I look forward to it every day. I thought dialoguing would be hard to do daily, especially on weekends because we always have company, but we make the time and it's been all worthwhile."

The team and priest giving the weekend give simple directions; they ask each couple to make a commitment to themselves to practice the dialogue daily. They even offer a guarantee: try it for ninety days and you will be committed for life. Some couples say, "Wow! The rest of my life—I can't think that far ahead." Yet for one couple in Queens, New York, "life" lasted only six weeks after the weekend. At his wife's wake the grieving husband could only thank heaven for the dialogue. It had given him a chance to say to her things he might never have expressed. A peaceful thread ran through his sadness; she had died knowing she was loved.

Allowing ourselves to be vulnerable to each other results in wonderment and awe and a growing trust. "I can honestly say there is a direct relationship between my spiritual growth and commitment to daily dialogue," said Father Bernie Pfau. "Our daily dialogue is the insured intimacy I have with Teresa that day," is the way Ron Fulmer sees it. "Regardless of what else happens, we have a special exchange which keeps us in sharp focus. We have an ever-renewable means to grow closer toward oneness."

Not everyone reacts favorably to the idea of practicing dialogue each day at home. "It sounded like another job to me," said Dom Esposito. Tom Kearns initially saw it as a "clever gimmick." Two years later he said, "Who would have thought it would be giving us even more than it did on the weekend?" Matt Ulrich shared how he thought the dialogue would be like "anything else. We would take it home, use it for a week and then pull it out later once in a while." But Matt found it became more and more a part of their life together. It was not just another gimmick. Any change in our lives is difficult to make, particularly one that must come through our own effort as opposed to one that is determined by circumstances beyond our control. It takes determination to live out a commitment to dialogue, and the commitment has to be renewed each day. Luk Adriaens explained that his wife, Mieke, pushed him into the weekend and afterward he had to push her into the daily dialogue. "Mieke," he claimed, "is more fantasy; she's against everything that is organized. But after five months I am proud to report we have a definite pattern."

"I was against daily dialogue at first," admitted Mieke. "But I know now it was because I thought other things were more important than Luk. Even in the beginning I realized that, but I didn't want to face it in myself because it meant changing habits I had built up."

The explanation of daily dialogue as presented by the team centers around an easily remembered acronym: WEDS for write, exchange, dialogue and select a question as dialogue topic for the following day. The slogan "10/10" refers to the time involved: ten minutes minimum for writing, ten minutes maximum for the verbal dialogue. The dialogue centers not around positions, attitudes, ideas, or decisions, but around feelings. "10/10 is a way of getting closer to one another every day," for Anne Moulton. She "finds it hard to be open to Ray but if I write I find it much easier."

Couples are encouraged to write their love letters in prime time; that is, the time when each is at his or her best. Too often we save only the tired time for each other. To avoid this trap, we ask couples to give each other ten minutes of their best time. If we want our relationship to grow to fullness, the letter cannot be fitted into just any convenient slot during the day.

The atmosphere in which the daily love letter is written is very important. Even though a couple is separated during the day, they are told to build up their awareness of each other consciously as they write. A beautiful side effect of the dialogue is that we know we are being thought of during the day. Even though couples may be separated from each other, each partner knows he or she is being remembered with love.

Betty Ann Connolly said, "It's one thing for Dave to call during the day just to say hello and tell me he's thinking of me—and I really look forward to those calls. But it's even better to know he is putting this special effort into building our relationship by writing a permanent record of his love and revealing an intimate part of himself. It makes me feel very much a part of his day." Marian Toner echoed this thought: "To me dialogue means knowing I'm in Jim's thoughts—that he's taking time out from all his pressures to tell me how special I am and how much I mean to him. Knowing this makes me feel loved and wanted and important to Jim—And when I take time out to think and picture him writing his love letter to me, it makes me yearn for him and his presence." Both of them know they are on each other's minds and in each other's hearts.

The "E" and "D" of WEDS—the exchange and dialogue—should be in "prime couple time," a time when husband and wife have ten minutes to spend for each other while they are fresh. The exchange of books should not be casual or mechanical. Couples are reminded to create an atmosphere of loving exchange of precious gifts, remembering that it is not just information in the notebook but an unveiling of part of the person one most dearly loves.

Many dialoguing couples have instructed their children to take over the house during dialogue time or to answer the phone, hoping their child will not reply as one did, "Mom and Dad are in the bedroom and won't come out." Even small children can be taught to respect these few minutes of private couple time. One couple, the Ferraras, let their preschooler be part of the exchange. "We usually give him an old notebook," Frank said. "He prays with us, and pretends he's reading. Then we ask him to go off and play quietly for ten minutes. Most of the time he cooperates well." Terry and Sheila Holly have teen-agers who take over: "They ask us in the evening if we've dialogued. If we haven't they send us off to do it." The Wallaces report a similar reaction: "When our children saw what the 10/10 meant to us, they were proud and wanted to help. They would answer the phone and take messages, and our oldest daughter would take care of the baby and try to keep the other children quiet. When we started the daily dialogue, we really didn't realize all the good effects it would have on us and on our children."

The whole purpose of the daily dialogue, as with the dialogue on the weekend, is to experience the other and allow the other to experience me. Our temptation is often to say "What are we going to do about this?" or "How are we going to fix this up?" but in the dialogue it is the feeling and, via the feeling, the person that we get to know. For the time being, problems do not have to be solved. The actual dialogue following the exchange and reading of love letters centers around the responsive feeling of one of the spouses—how one or the other of us is feeling in response to what was written.

As the verbal dialogue requires concentration and intensity, ten minutes is the suggested maximum. If the couple truly focuses on transplanting the feeling, the time flies by, tempting them to continue. But the experience of thousands of couples testifies to the wisdom of stopping after ten minutes are up.

Practiced over a period of time, the dialogue gives a husband and wife a tremendous sense of coupleness and a sensitivity to each other most would not have thought possible. The love letters and dialogue often stimulate ongoing discussion so that more and more the focus of their lives becomes "us."

Selecting a topic for dialogue the following day—the "S" of WEDS—keeps us aware of where we are in relationship to each other. The questions should be pertinent and personal. They should help us discover who we are. *Sex, death, possessions* and *God* are often good areas from which to choose questions. Also, subjects we frequently discuss as well as those we prefer to avoid usually point to the presence of strong feelings within us. Pat Bell calls it the "cement" of their relationship. "I realize fully that our closeness comes from daily dialogue and without it all my fears of myself and being open to Kathy would return to make me much less a person than I am."

"We choose a question that is important to us at the time," said Kevin Smith. "And to keep the dialogue alive in us all day, we try to pick the question right after dialogue." Selecting the question has more than the practical effect of being prepared for tomorrow; it is a continued commitment to a love relationship. Dialogue is a daily reminder of our care for each other. Like watering a plant, it produces steady growth. It helps couples be "the couple they are called to be," as Barbara Hannan stated in discussing the effects for Larry and herself. "I don't want the walls of privacy to invade our lives again," she added. "Because I love being a lover." Wally Matson said it this way: "Our dialogue is the tool that keeps us in tune with each other so we can share our music with the world."

Music, magic—this chance to keep it all alive is really the core of the Marriage Encounter. It is not the presentations themselves on the weekend or the atmosphere of the retreat house that brings this life. It is the couple becoming more open, more responsive. So on Sunday afternoon they pack their bags and regretfully leave the warm atmosphere of the retreat house, bidding a fond farewell to the couples with whom they have experienced the weekend, knowing they will probably never see many of them again. They say good-bye and thanks to the teams who shared the substance of themselves, their personhood and their coupleness.

The teams, the other couples are left behind. But one thing each couple who leaves the retreat house keeps is their notebooks —those precious treasures they will take home to become yellow with age and worn from being thumbed through.

"When we came back from our weekend," said Luke McSherry, "we held our notebooks in awe. They were treasured and revered almost as much as we treasured each other. We took these books into our bedroom and secreted them as if they were an intimate exposure of our life. They are still secreted, like a very personal and private exposé of our life together, almost like a secret diary of the life and love of Luke and Barbara."

"Our notebooks are precious to us," Sandy Schulteis said. "We have often reread them to bring back the memory of a beautiful weekend." "They are special in the way pictures in an album bring back happy memories," echoed Jimmy Manfredi. "I can tell you where we keep them. In a kitchen cabinet over the stove. Every time I open that cabinet there's a *ping!* that goes off inside of me."

Those notebooks will provide a reminder, a motivation, an urgency to write each successive day on the blank pages left. There are other notebooks to be bought and filled, a growing diary of each couple's love. Our daily dialogue becomes our daily prayer, our personal scripture. It will be the "good news" of Jesus Christ according to Arthur and Elsa, Cindy and Dick, Joe and Judy, Tom and Anne. Everything we discovered about one another, all the goodness, gentleness, tenderness, love and worth inside each of us was always ours. The gift of the weekend was simply a beautiful way to let it unfold.

CHAPTER XI

Developing the "10/10" Habit

Sunday afternoon started us thinking what it would be like when we got home. We were close, so close, to one another that Sunday and we never wanted to lose that experience so we were glad we could bring the dialogue home with us. It offered permanence and hope.

But back home is a different story. It is awfully easy to settle for a better relationship than we had before—one that has been improved so greatly by our experience of the weekend that a couple of weeks or a few months later we're not all that sure we want to pay the price of living up to the full potential of our relationship every day. There's a temptation to say "Why *every* day?" and the simple unanswerable response is "Why *not?*" Don't worry about tomorrow. Just dialogue today. And when tomorrow comes, that's another today.

Most of us tend to be a little careless, easily satisfied, as long as things are going well. It's only when there's a problem or a difficulty that we pay all that much attention. Daily dialogue is a positive program for growth, a commitment to stretch in our relationship, to build our love to its maximum potential, to grow more deeply in love with one another.

We human beings are masters at responding to fire alarms. In any home the children, the job, the neighbors, the problems of the world all tend to clang much more loudly than the couple. Unless a husband and wife deliberately and consciously, on a daily basis, put their concentration on each other, their relationship tends to come last. Yet Scripture tells us, "Out of the abundance of the heart, the mouth speaks." What flows from the abundant heart is the joy Our Father intends for us.

"Joy is being free to be myself," wrote Jack and Irene Callaghan. "Before dialoguing, so many of our moments of joy were private . . . little joys that seemed too unimportant to interest the other, or only partially shared joys, as when the children came home with a good paper from school or when we finally caught up on our bills. Often we recognized a glow of pleasure in one another, but shared only our thoughts and judgments. It was like making contact with one finger rather than the whole hand. . . . In sharing our feelings joy suddenly opens up like a flower. . . . And joy, like love, spills over."

Just as the weekend is not designed to correct a weakness, so too the daily dialogue is not intended to deal with a lacking but to build on strength. It is not aimed at those who cannot get along without it, but is a gift for those who love more *with* it.

One of the exciting things about the daily dialogue is that it is not something needed by the couple. Rather, they *deserve* their dialogue. Before they came on the weekend, most couples had a good marriage, loved one another and communicated well. The dialogue serves all these purposes—but its greatest value comes from revealing the beauty that is in each person. There is nothing ordinary about this beauty. It is unique, and we can never plumb its depths. Oona Olsen compared use of daily dialogue to stoking a fireplace: "You can sit in front of a fireplace feeling so warm and close, yet you still have to get up and poke around at the fire to keep it going. The same is true with our relationship. We have to keep it going with the dialogue."

A number of people from their church had come to Jim and Irene O'Rourke and urged them to go on this fabulous weekend. They had shared a lot together before their Marriage Encounter weekend, but Irene still had the feeling that somewhere along the line something was missing. "It was tucked under something and had been mislaid," she said. "When we were first married I remember feeling very special. I knew Jim loved me over the twenty-five years we were married, but in the beginning of our marriage I was very conscious of the fact that he loved me, thought me special, just by the way he'd look at me and touch me. You know, with the kids and the problems that come up, Jim's job, and the commitments we felt we had to have, the Scouts, the whole bit, we lost something. My hope was that that weekend would give us back whatever it was that got shuffled under all those things. On the weekend, I felt it coming back. When I started to dig and discovered how unsure and uncertain I was and shared it with Jim, he kept saying, 'I know.' But I kept saying, 'You don't know. You really don't know.' I discovered so much of me that weekend that I didn't even know about myself. Before those forty-four hours were over we had gotten back what was missing. It was the most beautiful weekend of our lives."

Werner and Frits Van Reusel expressed the warmth daily dialogue brings to relationship in another way: "Without it we saw that the sun of the weekend would soon turn to winter."

Daily dialogue is not just a practice, it is an expression of our commitment to *us* which leads to a sense of purpose and direction, and a realization of the value of the present moment, this minute, this hour, this day—the full value.

"Our daily dialogue is a gift, a blessing, a daily reminder of our commitment to each other, of how deeply we love each other and of how the Father loves us. It's our means to growth. It means living instead of existing. It means a whole new way of life, of purposeful giving, meaningful and loving. And to us it means living our Father's plan for us. I wouldn't give it up, because of what we experienced on our weekend. I want to love as fully as I can and I want to be loved, because of the joy and true peacefulness we've experienced." This is the way it was expressed by Pat Etner.

There is no question that the Encountered couple and priest have their homework to do if they are not to leave the weekend back at the retreat house. They have deliberately and consciously to concentrate on each other, looking closely at their relationship, or they will miss the totalness life offers.

The results of dialogue have been so varied and so positive that it would take a book in itself to record the reactions of the different couples. To Mary Ann Billeci the dialogue gave them "a time during the day when we sit down and we think about one another and really talk to each other. This is something we've never had before. We chit-chatted. We had never really talked about how we felt. Now, we have a way and a means to understand, and through this it grows and grows." The results are usually very simple, very plain. For Lucille Morgin "material things just aren't that important any more. Our dialogue is the most important part of the day. What really matters is Lowell." To others the decision to dialogue freed them once and for all from having to make that choice each day, between things and one another.

Unfortunately, there are so many ways of avoiding "life." There is the peace-at-any-price attitude. In any couple relationship we tend to say the things that please the other person, thinking, "Well, I'll get over it—this difficult feeling inside." We handle it ourselves instead of as a couple. It is the kind of peace, as Father George Murphy said so often, we find in cemeteries. We can afford it when we are dead.

None of us likes to be upset so we try not to cause waves. We don't want to say or do anything that would cause the other to be irritated or worried or depressed. So we tiptoe around each other a lot. Furthermore, even after the Encounter, we try to talk each other out of our feelings. We don't want the other person to feel badly for both our sakes—for our spouse's—because we honestly care about him and want him to be happy, and for our own, because we know we won't be at peace as long as the other is disturbed. Daily dialogue helps us immeasurably as a practical means to overcome our tendency to avoid certain subjects.

The normal routine and pattern of our day doesn't change as a result of making a Marriage Encounter weekend. There's still the job, the house, the children. We still have just as many bills to pay; the kids have to be chauffeured and homeworked; the television set still works, and so on. So it would be easy enough for us to fall back into our old way of relating to one another and think we were so different because we had made a Marriage Encounter. It's always so easy for us to kid ourselves and be much more involved with things and other people than each other. So we know that yesterday's dialogue was great for yesterday. Today is another day. That's the only day we have to live. It's today's love, not the past or the future, we have to decide upon. Marriage Encounter is not a one-shot deal. It is not something wonderful that has happened and it's over with and we look back with fond memories. Marriage Encounter is for today. So we dialogue today because, as the saying goes, today is the first day of the rest of our lives. We can settle for that high level of accommodation, getting along with one another as the goal of marriage or we can shoot for the stars.

"Daily dialogue means knowing Frank not just as the guy I married but as the greatest person I know. It's knowing him thoroughly, being more sensitive to him every day. I always knew he was a lover and a sensitive person—but I didn't want to know any more," commented Ginger Purcell. "10/10 makes me want to know him more—it keeps building! He's always been easy to get along with—now he's exciting to get along with. It's peace and joy and knowing that the struggles we *do* have are worth it in the long run. I don't want to give up the excitement of it!"

Sometimes couples have gotten so much out of a weekend that it is difficult for them to conceive that there is more. They just want to enjoy what they have. Writing is a particular barrier. "Why can't we just talk?" is a frequent query. The response is that you can and do just talk. But dialogue demands writing.

My own personal experience supports my conviction that writing is important. As a Jesuit I was trained to stop whatever I was doing twice a day and just stand in the presence of my Father and look to see where I stood with myself and Him. This was a time for me to examine with Him the love He had given me to spend, to discover where I was holding back from people, where I was coasting a bit and how I could love more meaningfully. Rarely have I missed doing this. But a lot of times I've just gotten it in; it hasn't been on my best time. Sometimes it has been casual or routine. Part of the exercise is to write down a little record of where I find myself. This tends to be skipped. My attitude is "Why can't I just talk to Him in my mind? Why do I have to write it down?" A lot of reasons for the writing come to mind, but the simplest one is the most persuasive: it works better that way. It isn't that I'm a bad priest if I don't write; it's that I'm more when I do.

Daily dialogue works the same way. A couple doesn't have to write, they are just more open when they do. Their intensity and their awareness increase. They are less likely to be *talking at* and more likely to be *communing with* each other.

When we talk about daily dialogue we mean the same practice as we experienced on the weekend. It is a normal human tendency to look for shortcuts and we can easily fool ourselves into believing that because we've made a weekend we can now be open and honest and responsive to each other without using the technique the way it was given us. We sometimes think we can just sit down and talk and really be dialoguing. Actually all the reasons for writing on the weekend are present in spades back home—we talk off the top of our heads, interrupt one another verbally and nonverbally, get distracted, face issues rather than one another, make assumptions about what the other person is saying or what's behind it, try to change the other person and on and on. So we write. It works better that way and we are better that way—better to and for one another.

Probably the best advice given to a couple just off the weekend is "do it every day." After nearly six years of visiting couples who have come home from the weekend, Tony and Marguerite Bonner give them the same advice—just keep dialoguing every day. As Tony says, "There are no good or bad dialogues—you just do it or you don't." And Marguerite adds how they have been doing it for close to six years and it's been so good for them they see no end in sight.

During the courtship days, a boy and a girl are constantly on the lookout for things to give each other. Often they do not have all that much money, so the things they give are not expensive—just little mementos. But it is the gift of themselves to each other. It expresses their personhood, their love.

According to Paul and Fran Sobieski, "The gift of dialogue showed us how to deeply communicate our specialness. That's it! Specialness. That is the goal we are seeking. We believe the Father has divinely ordained the gift of daily dialogue to help us believe in our uniqueness. God be praised; we found the *more*."

As Paul and Fran point out with such enthusiasm, the most powerful effect of the dialogue is that it helps each spouse realize how lovable he or she is. Too often a poor self-image kills the spark of love, and it is difficult if not impossible to convince ourselves of our own goodness. But the person we love most in the world can go a long way in denting the armor of worthlessness we all wear at times.

Jacques Le Jour saw himself as a "failure" in many respects, "very much selfish, almost incapable of loving, a poor husband. I therefore tried to prove myself in my job." He said, "My aim was to become best there. Through dialogue, piece by piece, I dared sharing how I saw myself as that very poor type of man. But to my great astonishment, instead of rejecting me, Ging started to love me. This gave life to me and I started feeling better in my skin. Step by step, knowing I was loved by Ging, I realized I was not just that miserable type of man, but capable of loving."

For each couple the dialogue means something a little different. But always it brings closeness, warmth and growth.

One woman who found an inability to have children difficult to face in herself found her "worth and goodness through dialogue," and said she is little by little coming to believe in the "full fertility" of their couple love. Don Sautner called dialogue "part of our pilgrimage to our Father's Kingdom." For Kitty Bates it is "that little bit of fertilizer any plant needs." Denis Stemmle compared building a relationship without dialogue to "carving a piece of wood with a dull knife."

Couples who come to the weekend and take the dialogue home may have spent many years together or been married only a short time. It doesn't matter.

Hope is in the air. Hope instilled on the Encounter itself—that reintroduction to the discovery of love and our potential to grow as lovers—our love is limitless. We now have an opened horizon of what we can be. It gives us a sense of our own dignity. In striving to be one, ten minutes at a time, the couple becomes more and more part of one another with a deeper awareness of and responsiveness to one another.

Dialogue is a source of strength and growth in the priesthood of Father Tom O'Rourke. "I am filled with gratitude as I see the changes in my life because of it. There is really no way back for me. Sometimes I see the traces of my former aloofness and stubbornness but the dialogue is a guarantee of that growth in relationship to the Church."

Every human being is a mystery. We never know a mystery. It is revealed to us. We discover the reality behind the shadows and shades we find ourselves in. And on the weekend we look at the greatest mystery itself—the mystery of love. There is no such thing as a born lover. Love does not just occur. It is created. It is not something we do naturally. It is something we learn and earn. The commitment to daily dialogue is a commitment to make love happen today.

The Davidsons had been married only three months when they began the daily dialogue. Howie realized as a doctor he could easily devote all his time to work and shut Clara out completely. "Without dialogue I would have put work first and not known what happened to us," he said. But after twenty-five years of marriage, dialogue was no less important to Betty-June and Jomy

Zech. "We have grown more in the last two years than in all the other years we were married," they reported.

Daily dialogue really does have an effect on your whole life, as I can attest from personal experience. Before I used to work and pray and sweat to come up with good things for people to do, the correct directions for them to take. I strove with everything I had to discover adequate motivation to encourage them to do the right thing by one another. I hoped whenever I was with people to say enough good things and provide an atmosphere of warm approachability so that some of them would seek me out afterward for my help, guidance and direction on a continuing basis. The sign I looked for as a clue that I was getting through with a sermon, a talk, a lecture was for heads to nod in confirmation.

Now all I want is for couples to listen not to me but to each other. I believe with all my heart, if they truly love each other they will be good to all. If they are truly open, they will instinctively do the right things for one another. I don't look for them to seek me out for counsel and direction. If I have had a hand in getting them to be important to each other then I will always be valued and wanted whether we meet every week or once every two years. The sign I now look for to indicate to me that I'm striking a responsive chord is for them to look at each other in recognition and joy. Before I wanted their agreement with me, their nod that I was right. Now I want them to turn to each other to recognize the powerhouse of their love and to draw closer to each other. Before I wanted to give them something worthwhile, now I want to mirror their beauty back to them. Before I provided ideas and insights, now I try to reveal my awareness of them. If they walk out arm in arm, that means much more than their flocking around me telling me that I have said something insightful. So my whole focus in life has changed as a result of dialogue. It changed from doing everything I possibly could for people, trying to help them to lead a better life, to enjoying their love for one another, trusting and rejoicing in their goodness, loving them and feeling their love for me.

The practice of daily dialogue came from the tentative and often painful first steps of couples who, early in the Encounter, discovered that their lives grew richer with each dialogue. Without daily dialogue, they know the weekend would have been a fond memory, very vivid and moving, but still a memory. When they failed to dialogue, they saw their lives soon settle back into complacency. Their powerful experience faded just as the first flush of romance faded early in their marriage.

"Without our daily dialogue," states Aileen Stahl, "I guess our life would be the way it was about four years ago, nice and a lot of fun but with no real depth or meaningful goals. Without the dialogue, we would not have come to feel Christ's presence so strongly."

"For us it is not that easy as saying—well, all we will do is go back to the way we were four and a half years ago. The trouble is we can never go back to that happy good marriage because we have experienced more than just a good, happy relationship. We know the weekend was more than we expected—it not only gave us a memorable weekend, it gave us the bridge to get beyond the accepted norms of a good marriage. However, we burned that bridge and now can never return. It's like children who grow up never being able to return to their childhood, which they thought was so great. By the same token, who wants to go backwards" is the conviction of Jim Toner.

Mark Hudson finds it hard to imagine what life without dialogue would be like. "Judging from those times when Marion and I have missed," he said, "I think life would be very empty. At those times I find myself slipping back into my old shell. Marion and I have been dialoguing for almost two and a half years, and our awareness of each other is very keen. Maybe another way to say it is that dialogue for a long period of time brought the relief of putting on moccasins after wearing heavy boots."

For Don Paglia dialoguing is "the ribbon on a beautiful package; it keeps us together with the nice bow. It is a promise that we will never allow ourselves to grow apart. I don't look at it as an obligation, but rather as an opportunity."

"Our daily 10/10 to me is like a pipe line to each other and to God, a thread that can be strong and unbreakable nylon or thin and easily broken cotton, depending on what we put into it and how we go into it," said Mary Burke.

The thought of not dialoguing really gets to Mario Corzo. "Not sharing with Kae in our dialogue is like living in two separate worlds. Daily dialogue is to me my whole awareness of life, the air I breathe, the water I drink, my daily prayer to the Father, the sharpness of my senses, my life line to Kae. It keeps me alive for Kae, to receive her feelings and to give her mine to love her and make the most of our lives together."

One of the subtleties about daily dialogue is that if a couple doesn't dialogue they are not even aware there is anything to miss. Furthermore, even for those who practice it, frequently it isn't until they omit it for a day or two that they come to any real comprehension of how deeply meaningful dialogue is to them. Often it is only by getting a taste of distance that we realize how close we have been. That is why the teams on the weekend so earnestly ask each couple to try it for ninety days even if it takes them one hundred and eighty to do it. The teams know it is hard to get it going but they also know from their own personal experience as well as that of hundreds of their friends that once a couple really starts with it, that, as Susie Laing put it, "It changes the gray of life to a thousand brilliant colors."

The Encounter Family has learned that no one dialogues alone. As dialoguing couples grow in an awareness of each other, so too the technique of dialogue evolves. Insights are shared; ways of discovering feelings are exchanged. Renewal nights provide an opportunity for Encountered couples to share with one another. Every local Encounter community has a newspaper made up of couples' sharings to support and encourage the continuation of daily dialogue.

No matter where I went the words that kept coming up when I

asked people about their daily dialogue were: light, sun, life line. Whether in Los Angeles or New York, Ireland or Belgium, Minnesota or Louisiana, they spoke of growth, new life, no walls, freshness. It was simply amazing to hear people from all walks of life and such diverse educational backgrounds all talk the same way. Each had his own unique experience between the two of them and yet the result was common—warmth, closeness, coupleness.

Another benefit of the dialogue is knowing that we, as couples, are not alone. Literally tens of thousands of couples all over the world are growing in love every day. This experience builds up a sense of world-wide unity among the couples and priests. Couples everywhere—in the United States, Australia, in Belgium, British Honduras, England, Japan, Ireland, Taiwan, France, Mexico, Canada and India—are reaching out today to experience each other more deeply in exactly the same way. This gives each couple a sense of strength and value to the world, changing and softening their attitude toward all people. They feel a part of a world-wide family: couples and priests with whom they speak a common language.

There is a real security that comes with knowing that I speak the same language, that I have common experiences, common failings, common hopes, common ideals with people all over the world. It is an expansionary experience for people to know that they are more than themselves. They have the joyful knowledge that, should they ever travel to almost any place in the world, they have a family waiting. As soon as they land they can call people who do not even know their names, assured of being welcomed into their homes and hearts. It is a fascinating event to land in a strange city and be swept into the arms and love of a couple. Couples look forward to having their brothers and sisters stay, sitting up late into the night sharing their relationship and just being present to one another. It is a chance to discover how the family is growing in different parts of the world, and to encourage one another.

One of the real gifts of Marriage Encounter, in addition to revealing hidden resources a couple has within themselves, is to introduce them and to expose them to other couples of the same ideals and the same values. Furthermore, the common struggle these couples experience and share with one another in continuing their experience of Marriage Encounter through the practice of the form of communication taught them is a real encouragement for them to continue hoping and to continue reaching out for more in their relationships.

One of the beautiful effects of the dialogue is an increased awareness of God as a person with a tremendously tender love for us. All too often a husband and wife have an individual private relationship with God. He has his God and his relationship with Him and she her God and her relationship with Him. Through dialogue as they discover each other more they go to God together. It is their love for each other that most disposes them to be aware of God revealing Himself. God is love-persons in relationship. The couple is the greatest human experience of persons in relationship. The more they truly and deeply experience one another, the more conscious they become of God's presence. God speaks Himself—love. So when they most deeply and meaningfully love one another they are most disposed toward and capable of hearing and responding to God's revelation of Himself.

A number of years ago while I was at Gonzaga Retreat House for Youth, I used to tell the guys on retreat that sometimes the greatest gift God ever gives a man is five feet two, blond, blue-eyed, and built. By that I meant that they often would go to Mass or confession because of the girls they cared for. But now I realize it is so much deeper than that. Their relationship with one another disposes them to be aware of God present to them.

Marriage calls a man and woman to be fully open to each other to give and receive their personhood. It calls for a total and irrevocable commitment to find themselves in each other. *This* is fidelity. Fidelity is not two good people who live together doing the right thing by one another. Roommates do that. It is not a man and woman who are content with each other's company and who satisfy each other's needs. You don't have to be married for that. Marriage calls for a full faithfulness—a striving for total awareness. It's not simply balancing life-styles and working out a give-and-take arrangement that leaves both parties content. The aim is full integration, true oneness, complete involvement. We are not seeking partnership but coupleness. It is not easy. The goal is glorious but it demands constant attention to each other. Daily dialogue clears our vision, fine tunes our hearing, stretches our arms and strengthens our hearts. There is a Mona Lisa smile on the face of every dialoguing couple and priest spreading the worst kept secret in the world: "We dialogued today and we wish everyone did."

CHAPTER XII

Love Is a Decision

Marriage Encounter is not a drawing-board response to sociological patterns. It is people. Every couple gets married with certain ambitions centered around getting ahead and settling down. These may include a job with a future, frequent promotions, growth in income and maybe even security through a pension plan. Probably among the goals are a small house of their own, then a bigger house in a nice neighborhood. Plans for the house commonly include outfitting it in the best possible manner: washing machine, dryer, refrigerator, television, freezer, furniture, carpeting, drapes and so forth. They hope the children will be able to attend the best possible schools and have nice clothes, toys and recreational facilities. Looking further ahead, they want to prepare their children to achieve material success in life.

Most couples after a relatively few years of marriage are well on their way toward reaching these goals. Yet, even with all their early dreams basically fulfilled, something seems to be missing. A nagging dissatisfaction stirs inside them or, at best, they develop a case of the "blahs." Initially, their response may be to raise their sights in the same plane and seek more—more job, more car, more house, maybe even a summer house, more savings, more future security, more insurance. They increase their efforts to give their children the best by adding dancing classes, music lessons and exposure to various cultural activities. Still, it is not enough. They may turn to social events, recreation, entertainment, additional schooling, distractions of all kinds, filling their lives with going places and doing things. Others spend themselves in being active in various church and civic groups such as Confraternity of Christian Doctrine, politics or Little League. Still others pour themselves into their family, spending as much time as possible with the children. But nothing seems to fill that nagging void.

At this point, couples can't understand how they can have all they ever dreamed of and more and still not be satisfied. All that seems to be left is living out a meaningless life filled with unsatisfying obligations and responsibilities. They have little to look forward to.

Some couples who go on a Marriage Encounter go because they know that growth in relationship is the road to fulfillment. Others have simply sensed there is something wrong with the plan society expects them to live out. Searching for hope, we all want something to look forward to. We want the excitement of growth and the exhilaration of discovery—a sense of purpose. We may look back to our adolescence and young adult years when we had mighty dreams. As the dust of the years settles around us, many of us lose our ambitions, our dreams and acquiesce to the humdrum of daily life. We become more aware of our limitations and we may unconsciously adopt the attitude of the cynic who ceases to dream. Yet, the disappointment haunts us; we wanted to go to the mountaintop.

Too often a husband and wife lie side by side staring up at the ceiling, neither aware that the other is awake. Separately they ask themselves "What happened to our love?" Certainly they are not thinking of divorce or even of doing anything but the best they can by each other, but it is the cry of a lonely heart in the night. In a sense, they are saying to themselves "I am not who I thought I was; my spouse is not who I thought he or she was; and marriage is not what it is cracked up to be."

"People always told me we seemed to be so happy together," said Cathy O'Brien. "We *were* happy, but I felt at times there was something missing from our lives. We had few disagreements. Mike was always in a good mood and wanted to please me, and we each had some outside interests. I looked forward to

Mike's coming home to share my day. Mike is well-read, up on everything, and we had a lot to talk about. I couldn't pinpoint any problem, but I sensed there could be more than we had."

"We were in a rut," said Tom Toy. "Somehow the conversations about crab grass, vacations, office politics and the children just didn't add up to a satisfactory relationship."

In most cases the cause of the restlessness never really gets tackled, but it crops up in symptoms. The real disillusionment is masked as we deal with only surface irritations: the toothpaste tube squeezed in the middle, socks on the floor, grumbling over housekeeping or late hours at work, an empty gas tank, a busy signal on the phone.

"I remember how concerned I was during the first years together," reflected Mary Badinghaus, "when Ed would get up sick or coughing in the middle of the night. But after a while, those middle of the night interruptions annoyed me. I was also more easily irritated by the shoes that were left out, the crumbs that weren't cleaned up after a midnight snack."

"When we made our Marriage Encounter, we'd been married for twenty-nine years," responded the Martins. "As practicing Catholics we believed we had to work at our marriage. Our friends considered our marriage to be solid, one of the best around. In our spare time, we each sought self-fulfillment; and we tolerated each other's failures to live up to expectations. Sometimes we tolerated well, sometimes poorly, but always those failures were too unimportant to destroy our marriage. However, in later years we had developed a pattern that was becoming disruptive. We had begun to argue too often over unimportant issues with each of us trying to prove we were right."

Inside the heart of each and every one of us there is a longing to be understood by someone who really cares. When a person is understood, he can put up with almost anything in this world. Yet often this understanding is missing in marriage. Our confusion is further complicated by the fact that it isn't particularly fashionable to talk favorably about marriage unless we are honeymooners or celebrating a golden anniversary. We have so little experience in living together, and almost all the advice given to married couples is aimed at telling them how to lead separate lives. Comments such as "Don't let her lead you around" or "Show her who's boss" or "Everyone is entitled to a night out and a little fun" or "Don't get too tied down" or "Everyone should do his own thing" make couples wonder what they really should expect from marriage. The advice doesn't offer any help in growing together or developing a relationship. Properly followed, it leads a couple to become little more than compatible roommates. Yet, most couples really don't buy the cynicism about marriage. They may go along and tell the jokes, but deep in their heart, their marriage is precious to them. Most couples take pride in wanting a good and lasting marriage.

"Is this all my life is ever going to be?" Jan Rigdon said she often asked herself. "It seemed there wasn't much more than cleaning the house all the time, and I thought, who needs this; no wonder he goes on business trips. It scared the hell out of me that I didn't feel loving; and I wondered if we did love each other any more. Now I realize we did, we just didn't very often tell each other."

Bernadette Vetter was worried about the future: "I accepted the rut we were in; but I couldn't help wishing for more. I was afraid to think of what the future held for our relationship if we didn't have more control over it. I wanted more for our marriage, but I didn't know what or how to find it."

Some couples, to avoid conflict and keep disillusionment from surfacing, may settle for peace at any price—and often the "price" is a relationship. "If we disagreed, we didn't voice our opinion but buried it so it wouldn't cause an argument," Phil and Joyce Hoffman said. "We never discussed a lot of topics. Even though we went to church together we worshiped two separate Gods. We seldom talked about sex or death."

Looking to the years ahead and wondering what will come when the children are gone is another symptom of emptiness in our lives. Often couples who have made all sorts of sacrifices of time, energy and personal interests to prepare their children for the future find themselves asking "What is there for me when they're gone?" Much of their life has been spent in seeing that the kids become well-rounded people, get a good education and have fond memories of home. As the children grow older, the couple who has devoted so much to them may begin to feel aimless and wonder what is left.

"Instead of thinking there would be more time for us to be together now to do things we never did before, I felt shattered," recalled Mercedes Nola. "Tom would have his job to keep him busy, but I expected to be very lonesome."

Women may make plans to fill the anticipated gap in their lives and even look forward to having time to themselves. But as the time approaches, they may begin to realize it will take more than activities to fill the void.

"I was going to have a fulfilling career," said Connie Emry. "Because I knew for sure I didn't want to stop growing. In fact, one manifestation of our separateness was my preoccupation with growth. From that threshold—anticipating a return to teaching—I peered into the future—but reluctantly."

"I thought with the age the children were my job was finished," echoed Kathleen McDonnell. "The children didn't need us any more, and that was it. The weekend was everything for us."

It is the openness, the sheer radiance of couples who have made a Marriage Encounter that excite so many others to go. Attracted by what Father George Wolfe called "the magnetism of the couples," couples see something they want for themselves. Like Father Wolfe, they want to see "what caused this glow."

And what they find is simply a weekend that addresses itself to that undiscussed, unprepared-for state in life called relationship. There is no way to measure what happens to couples on the weekend; it is a deeply personal experience. Whether large or small, barriers come down, romance comes alive and couples feel free to be themselves. Afterward couples are eager to talk about the new "us." Their disillusionment often passes into joy as the feeling of love becomes attached to a decision to be open and couples begin to live again in the presence of each other.

"I wondered why we were so happy before we got married," recalled Frank Gilchrest. "It was because the focus was on Diane and not Frank. That's what happened on the weekend. I put the focus back on Diane. One of the hardest things I did was to tell her how much I needed her."

Another couple called the experience of the weekend an "awakening to the secret parts of us." Often we live in the future, making plans for what will be, asking "How can we educate the children, prepare for retirement, spend the next vacation or the next night out? We wonder what's ahead, if he or she will change, and if not, if we'll be able to continue coping. Or we may look over our shoulders, reliving the past, remembering the last vacation or the last night out or the way we were back then. As a result, we miss most of the opportunities to just enjoy the goodness of each other. As we worry about improving our lives, we fail to see the beauty in front of us. But the only time we can have a relationship with each other is in the present moment; the only time we can love each other is *now*."

"Marriage Encounter restores the vision of closeness. I had dreamed of sensitivity and closeness with Pat," Kathy Bell recalled. "Sharing our souls, goals and joys. The weekend gave us a way to communicate what was going on inside of us. We thought after marriage that came automatically, but often we found we couldn't share. We began to see the beauty we had when we first married and thought would last a lifetime but had dulled."

The results were summed up very briefly by Fred and Kay Weiss: "We'll never be the same again."

Each person in this world—every one of us—has a tremendous capacity for love. But despite the love stored up and buried within us, there doesn't seem to be much outlet for it. Oh, we may find all sorts of opportunities to *do* things; but love is restricted when it is confined to doing. Love is not an interchange of good deeds done for each other; it is an interplay of persons who belong to each other, not in the possessive sense of the word but in the sense of having roots and identity in one another, in being a part of one another's lives.

When the doubtful, the cynical and even the believers ask "Will it last? Will the joy of the weekend fade away?" we can only reply: Love is a decision. This single insight opens up a whole new world for us, because whether we realize it or not, we often act on the assumption that love is a feeling. Feelings accompany love; they are not the love itself. They are generated by openness and responsiveness to another person. When we really listen to each other and sense a new understanding between us, feelings of warmth, tenderness and gentleness can very well be present. The statement a couple is asked to make to the Church at the time of marriage is "I will." This is not the future tense of the verb "to be" but the old Latin verb "*volo*" meaning "I choose" or "I decide." For most couples, fully realizing that love is a decision—that we have the power at any given moment to commit ourselves to another—brings hope. We are no longer subject to the vagaries of our feelings. We can always choose to be responsive because that's what love is—a response.

When this discovery hits couples on the weekend, they express their excitement in different ways.

"To me it meant we didn't have to cope with the Hollywood vision of walking forever into the sunset any more," was how Grace DiFrisco saw it. "We aren't always going to be Robert Young and Dorothy McGuire. I can make the decision without waiting for all the violins and harps to be playing. It was like having a burden lifted to realize that love was my decision and not something that was going to fly in the window." Fritz Schaeffer compared hearing that love is a decision to "being taken by the scruff of the neck and shaken. We knew what we wanted in our marriage, but we didn't think we had much control over being bored with each other," he said. "We thought that was a part of life. Suddenly we saw we could control it just by sharing more of ourselves."

Toni Hess said, "The weekend shook me out of waiting for something to happen. It said, 'It's up to you; get going.'"

"It took away all my loopholes," admitted George Sullivan. "I had thought of love as a nebulous thing you either did or didn't have. I realized if I don't make that decision to be open, I can't blame anyone but myself."

Marriage Encounter is both traumatic and evolutionary. As a weekend it knocks us off our horse and wakes us up to where we are. As a process it develops our new consciousness and heightens it more and more.

Dialogue is cumulative in its effects on our relationship. But the only dialogue that is important is today's. It is an external manifestation of how close we yearn to be to each other during this twenty-four-hour period. We're going to set aside this special time just for our love. Just for this brief period of time each day, everything else stops—it is time for us. Too often we can postpone really talking to one another because so many other things need to be done right now. We have the best will in the world; we really intend to spend some real time together each day, but the day just seems to slip away from us. Daily dialogue helps us to put us first at least for that ten-minute period each day. It helps us keep our priorities straight. We find when we do put us first all the other things that are important get done. But if we put the other things first all too frequently we end up being squeezed out. Marriage Encounter is not an event, not something done to us. It is simply being more aware and responsive to one another.

CHAPTER XIII

Changing the World

Neither arms nor butter nor political power will change the world. Couple love will change the world. I believe that and tens of thousands of others, among them priests, nuns, brothers and married couples, believe it too. In our opinion Marriage Encounter offers more hope for the present and the future than anything else on the horizon.

When couples on the weekend hear the team couple say "We are going to change the world," they are sometimes taken aback. In the pause that follows, an electricity seems to crackle in the room.

A couple who has made a Marriage Encounter has experienced the real power generated by two people loving each other. They may have always known in theory that love is powerful. But as a result of the weekend they have felt that power. At first they are aware only of the impact their openness has had on each other; but when the team mentions changing the world, they begin to focus outward and see the potential joy that can be brought to others.

For some couples, the experience of the weekend has been so overwhelming that they find it easy to accept the possibility of their helping to create a more beautiful world. "I can remember on our first weekend," Brenda Hager said, in describing her reaction to the idea of changing the world, "realizing we had always loved each other but were stagnating because we had been keeping too much to ourselves. I was jumping up and down in my excitement, saying to Skip, 'Can't you see—we really can change the world. There's a reason to be married. There's a reason for us.' I was excited and enthusiastic about our specialness and importance to others—perhaps for the first time."

Others are more reserved in their initial reception of the idea. But later, after experiencing daily dialogue at home and the trust and openness of the Marriage Encounter Family, they find themselves realizing the possibility it offers for a changed world. As Father Roger De Vleeschouwer explained it, "I can remember hearing the words with astonishment and skepticism. To change the world had been my dream when I became a priest, but after experiencing disillusionment, I wasn't as ready to believe it could happen. But in my first experience of the Marriage Encounter Family after the weekend, a visit with an Encountered couple, I realized I had never been accepted by people in the way I was accepted by them. They shared so deeply in such a real way that I began to believe in our power to change; and this belief has continued to grow."

When Encounter teams speak of changing the world, we are not speaking as outsiders but as members of a family who recognize the good that is there but see that the quality of living can be improved with love and effort. We do not see ourselves as better in any way but only as people with something vital to share. We aren't going to give the world anything it doesn't already have but only provide the opportunity for other couples and priests to know more fully their own richness. We share the excitement of a pioneer who knows his discovery will have a lasting impact not just on himself but on all society.

In the past we so often looked to economics or education or political structures to improve the quality of our life. This hasn't been very successful, but we keep hoping. We create massive agencies and organizations to solve the problems of our society. We organize drug rehabilitation centers, prison reform groups, civil rights agencies, antiwar efforts. But it seems that no sooner have we solved or faced into one problem than another bigger one crops up. These crises that we spend so much time trying to solve are only symptoms. They divert our attention and energy from finding and treating the cause.

Much of the frustration in life and the lack of genuine fulfillment is a result of having the wrong goals. A doctor I know put it into perspective one day after attending a medical convention. The speaker there had pointed out that if cures were discovered for the three major killers in the United States—arteriosclerosis, heart disease and cancer—it would add seven years to the average life expectancy of Americans. As the doctor listened, he wondered what American people would do with those seven years. What would extra time be worth to them? Probably very little unless they love and are loved.

Love isn't something everyone needs in his personal life so he can do better in real life. Our real life is our love life. Instead of leaving love up to poets and songwriters, social workers or religious leaders, why not recognize that love is up to us and that it alone can change the world?

I hear people say "Life is real, life is serious." "We have to make a living," they insist. "We have to provide for the future, take care of our children, look to the needs of society." Granted these may be important, but should they be so all-embracing that we bypass the whole purpose of life?

In the real world married people live with their husband or their wife. Real life begins with that relationship and not in the factory or the conference room or in a thousand recreational pursuits so often undertaken to escape facing the emptiness we sense at home. All too often only at the death of our spouse do we realize how much we cared and what we missed.

Unfortunately, most of our plans for change fall within the same set of values we've always had. What we need is a radical change. To look beyond the pattern we are in. To break out of our box. Too often we are making the box bigger or more comfortable when our real freedom depends on throwing it away.

What couples envision is the kind of change Jesus talks about in the Gospels as they see that love is not an abstraction, not a feeling, not sentimentality, but a creative force that can be produced by a lived-out decision to be open and responsive. The message of the Gospels suddenly becomes personalized for many couples on the weekend; they realize that God is very much alive in them and that the Scriptures are more than unattainable ideals.

Nearly every couple who goes on a Marriage Encounter has sensed something missing in their life, but most had thought or hoped that the improvement depended on a change in circumstances. "If only he had a better job," they think, or "If she were tied down less with children and had more time for her own interests." Or they may blame it on family problems, or lack of education, or lack of freedom or "the system." Or maybe they realize the "something missing" is more personal than that. They may even be aware of a lack of depth in communication, but be resigned to what they think is the lot of all married people. After the weekend couples say, "Hey—wait a minute—if love can do this to us—it can do it to everyone. If we can change so much—why not the rest of the world?"

Priests have been pretty much in the same boat as couples. We have looked for our circumstances to change; "If only we weren't so tied down," or "If the system would change," or "If we could have a different assignment" or "If people would demand a little less and remember a bit more." We may realize we have to be different but we don't know how. Then Encounter comes along and helps us to see that our priesthood is not so much what we *do* for people but who we *are* to them. Bishop Edward McCarthy captured the whole rejuvenating spirit of the Encounter for priests when he said, "Before Marriage Encounter they kissed my ring. Now they kiss me."

This whole idea of changing the world seems so grandiose, doesn't it? There are so many conflicting forces in this world, so many massive, mind-boggling problems, so many opposing interests. How could you ever even dream of coping with them? You're right, we can't possibly come to grips with such things.

We're not trying to face problems, we're reaching out to people. We don't intend to give them anything or get anything from them. We just want to let them blossom. We trust in them. Once they experience their individuality and coupleness in its fullness, then everything else will fall into place.

You say "That's nice but it won't work." Give Marriage Encounter a chance. All the other schemes and plans and hopes haven't gotten us anyplace. Back in the early days of the Marriage Encounter we were only a handful and I was trying to persuade priests to get involved in the Encounter. We priests were pretty cautious. We've seen and tried all sorts of programs and experiences, that seemed so grand at the start, collapse under us and fade away. Consequently many of my brothers used to say to me "How can you be so sure? What if Marriage Encounter shoots up and then tails off?" I said then and would still say, "I know in my heart it works. It really brings the Lord's joy to people's lives. And it's *big*. It can have a world-wide impact. I know this in the depths of my soul. But you may be right. I can't give you a guarantee, I'm not infallible. Maybe five years or ten years from now it will have had its day, but in the meantime we will have had a helluva ride."

As a result of the closeness they experience in that short forty-four-hour period of a Marriage Encounter, couples become aware, often with a greater intensity than ever before, of how much they care for each other, of how much they have within themselves to share, of the potential for joy in their own relationship. Nothing has changed—they are still the same people—but because they have faced themselves and each other and seen the beauty there, their world has changed. From this experience comes the recognition of how available the power they have discovered is to every good marriage, so that changing the world seems almost a logical next step.

Once we have made a weekend, our lives are so touched that they are forevermore changed. It is a rare couple who goes on Marriage Encounter and leaves the weekend without a real stirring in their hearts and a chanting in their soul because the world is different. On returning home they very quickly see that their love naturally overflows to others. Two people who have learned to be sensitive to one another are naturally more sensitive to others as well—children, friends, neighbors and even acquaintances.

The danger here, of course, is that in rediscovering each other a couple can withdraw into a sort of isolationism. As long as my love for my spouse is O.K. and I am loved by him or her then everything's O.K. But it is not. What we are talking about is that couple love is a resource to be spent on the whole world—an opportunity for all men to know that they are good, loved and lovable.

Couples usually find a heightened responsiveness to their children as anxiety about the children's future is replaced by enjoyment of the present. In the homes of dialoguing couples I have seen walls come down and spontaneity and warmth fill the distances that had separated family members. The emphasis in our conversations in the past used to be on activities and interests, but now they center on getting to know one another as people, explaining feelings. Encounter parents are more likely to want to know what is going on inside their children than what they did at school that day.

John and Donna McGuire made their weekend "to have time to devote just to each other for a whole weekend and deepen our relationship. This came out of our Marriage Encounter, but so much more than we ever even dreamed could happen grew from it. Our family became so much closer to us and each other. We are all so much more aware of each other. We see our children as real people with lives of their own, not just as our possessions or as someone to give orders to, and expect them to comply with what we want."

Another reason the notion of changing the world becomes viable is that significant reconciliations have taken place within families and neighborhoods of couples who made the Encounter.

One man on the Sunday night of his weekend went up to his brother with whom he hadn't spoken for ten years and hugged him.

But the vision goes beyond the individual couple spending their new awareness on those around them and on communities coming together. It isn't just because we change one by one that the whole world will eventually change. It has more impact than that. There is a tremendous desire within couples who have experienced Marriage Encounter to have everyone experience the weekend or, at least in some way, to help unleash everyone's capacity to love and be loved.

Reconciliation with all individuals is needed. We must come together in the Church. All too often we have related to one another in terms of functions rather than as persons. We have forced some into isolated loneliness and reacted to issues and positions rather than responding to the personhood of others.

I had a tremendously exhilarating experience standing in a basketball arena surrounded by couples and priests and watching a man stopped dead still by the applause rained down upon him. It was especially significant because this particular man had had many years of practice at public events and had schooled himself well to be impassive. He was used to being treated impersonally, even with distaste, and knew how to accept the politeness of controlled applause. But this was different. He sensed that we were telling him we loved him, and that old man wasn't used to that. He was a bishop.

We want everyone to go on Marriage Encounter, not because Marriage Encounter is so great, but because each person is. We don't want to give others what they lack but put a spotlight on how grand they already are. As we did that bishop, we accept the challenge of anyone who says they are already fully aware of the richness of their marriage. We merely say "Come and see."

Couples who are excited about Marriage Encounter are excited because they realize how lucky they are to have learned before it was too late how much they do care for and appreciate the beauty in one another.

Teams such as Jerry and Judy Cirou sometimes find "the excitement of our vision is overpowering—skyrockets and firecrackers and stars twinkling and joy—joy—joy bursting in our hearts."

It is a vision of a world changed in love—we thought for so long it was the impossible dream. It is not impossible—we know that now—our experiences of the weekends are all the proof we need. On those weekends we often can't sleep on Friday night— there's too much excitement building. Saturdays there is love growing—budding—blooming—and by Sunday there are tears of joy and smiles and more tears and more joy. The impetus is very simple and very basic—it's the realization that I am a lovable person—that God made me uniquely who I am. He loves me so much that He gave me my spouse to share life with. On that weekend we ask our couples to look at each other—to absorb the beautiful gift of each other—to accept our Father's love, and to share that love with others. How often we've complicated it and stumbled along wondering who we are and where we are going. Keep it simple—yes, and when we do—we can envision a world growing in love—people opening up and reaching out—young people and old people side by side. A little love goes such a long way. So there doesn't have to be a generation gap—nor families torn and hurting. But because there is understanding and love changing our world, someday guns will be melted and wars dissolved. We can see our Father's kingdom growing.

With a strong urgency within us to spread the good news, few sacrifices are too great to keep us from giving the weekend wherever there are interested couples. The basic principle within Marriage Encounter continues to be: "Give us twenty couples and we will send a team anywhere in the world whatever the cost."

The Encounter had been going for about a year in Dublin when couples there got a request to introduce Encounter into

Belfast. Naturally, they were very frightened about doing it. Yet
at the same time they felt a sense of obligation deep in their
hearts that they couldn't turn down their Northern Irish
brethren, most particularly because they were in such difficult
straits and living in such terror. Yet there was that fear in them,
and not even just for themselves, but more for their children. So
the couples that were chosen to go to Belfast as teams sat down
with their families before they said "Yes" and explained the
whole situation to the children and then asked them if they could
go. They explained very carefully and very truthfully that it
might well be that they might not come back. They asked
whether the children would be willing to have them go. All the
children of those team couples responded, "Don't you dare not
go!" So they went. They went up to the border and they changed
into a car with Northern Irish license plates because they
thought there might be less trouble from the guards and from the
English soldiers. They were stopped and searched eight times on
the way. One of the women in the car, while the others were
being questioned, happened to look out the other side of the car
and saw thirty soldiers lying down in the field with machine guns
pointed at them. During the course of the weekend, on Saturday
afternoon, they heard some explosions and on Sunday, rifle fire.
But they went back, and went back again. Now they're giving an
Encounter every month in Belfast, and by the time this book is
published, there should be close to three hundred Encountered
couples in Northern Ireland.

The team couples are not fanatics, nor are they motivated by a
desperate escape from some disastrous marital situation. They
had good marriages before the weekend. It is not being rescued
from matrimonial death that moves them; it is the more abundant life that they can't keep to themselves.

Marriage Encounter is an opportunity for couples who really
love one another to make their good marriages great. It begins
with a weekend exposure to, and experience of a technique of

communication that heightens their awareness of, and sensitivity to one another. It is a real fountain of youth for love, restoring the glow to their relationship that they had when they first married. Marriage Encounter gives husband and wife pride, and enthusiasm in being a couple.

People not familiar with Marriage Encounter must often wonder what attracts couples and priests to the movement. How could we be so eager to spread the Encounter unless there was something in it for us. In a sense, we do have much to gain: a better world, a world where people know that to live is to love. But our aim is not to get couples excited about Marriage Encounter but to get them excited about each other. We want people to make a weekend not because they need one but because they deserve one. Hopefully, Marriage Encounter is a specific moment of grace in the life of the Church. It is an occasion for couples in this period of time to come to a deeper relationship with one another. It calls us to be more for one another. The strength of Marriage Encounter lies only in the individual day-by-day absorption in one another by each husband and wife.

Perhaps most important is that Marriage Encounter people haven't given up on the world, because the world is all of us. So much of the world we live in is callous and exploitative that it may come as a shock that total strangers should care about you, the reader. This is difficult to believe and to accept but maybe reversing the old saying "All the world loves a lover" to "The lover loves the whole world" can make it credible. That is what Marriage Encounter people are trying to be—lovers. Lovers first and foremost of one another, and then of everyone that they meet and come in contact with. We have only one gift that we can share with you, and that is ourselves. We believe in you and we believe in your earnest desire to love one another. Furthermore we want to experience your love and be enriched by it.

If the world is to be changed through Marriage Encounter, couples are needed who are willing to experience the forty-four-hour weekend. The worst thing that can happen is that nothing happens. They go home the way they came. On the other hand, there is the possibility that a whole new world will open up. So it's a gambler's bet. Who can afford not to take it?

ENJOY!

Afterword

The following people are quoted throughout the book. They are part of the worldwide Encounter community, which has made this book possible.

Adriaens, Luk & Mieke	Louvain, Belgium
Atkinson, Sandy & Jack	Clinton, New York
Badinghaus, Ed & Mary	Cincinnati, Ohio
Bates, Kitty	Dublin, Ireland
Beattie, Mike	Exton, Pennsylvania
Bell, Pat & Kathy	Rochester, New York
Benjamin, Jim & Joan	Columbia, Maryland
Berrigan, Pat	Slidell, Louisiana
Billeci, Mary Ann	Pittsburg, California
Bonner, Tony & Marguerite	Montclair, New Jersey
Brendese, John	Troy, New York
Brennan, Ann	Los Angeles, California
Brewster, Pat	Brentwood, New York
Brown, Roz	Renton, Washington
Buisson, Ralph & Merce	Gretna, Louisiana
Burke, Harry & Mary	Dayton, Ohio
Buzzoni, Buzz & Dee	Purcellville, Virginia
Callaghan, Jack & Irene	Wexford, Ireland
Capretta, Don	Pleasanton, California
Chicavich, Madeleine	Queens, New York
Christiansen, Richie & Penny	Hicksville, New York

Ciecuich, Bernadette	Oyster Bay, New York
Cinege, Joe & Cindy	Lakewood, New Jersey
Cirou, Jerry & Judy	Mesa, Arizona
Clark, John	Lakewood, California
Coffey, Phil	Floral Park, New York
Connolly, Dave & Betty Ann	Upper Montclair, New Jersey
Cooper, Annette	Sydney, Australia
Coppi, Dave	Stonybrook, New York
Corzo, Mario	Houma, Louisiana
Davidson, Howie & Clara	New Orleans, Louisiana
DeBlasio, Skip	Huntington, New York
Del Rey, Diane	Staten Island, New York
De Vleeschouwer, Father Roger	Brussels, Belgium
DiFrisco, Grace	Medinah, Illinois
Donnelly, Joe	Dublin, Ireland
Doucette, Phil & Brunhilde	Livingston, New Jersey
Dugas, Pam	New Orleans, Louisiana
Duphiney, Mary	Parsippany, New Jersey
Dwyer, Phil	Sudbury, Canada
Elser, Duane	Los Alamitos, California
Emry, Fred & Connie	Coeur D'Alene, Idaho
Ennis, Tommie & Ann	Dublin, Ireland
Esposito, Dom	Garden City South, New York
Etner, Pat	Waldwick, New Jersey
Ferrara, Frank & Linda	Brooklyn, New York
Finn, Nancy	San Mateo, California
Flaherty, Art	West Orange, New Jersey
Florio, Ralph	Brooklyn, New York
Fuerst, Richie & Joan	Croton-on-Hudson, New York
Fulmer, Ron & Teresa	San Mateo, California
Gee, Ken & Julia	Sydney, Australia
Genovese, Dolores	Mamaroneck, New York
Genovese, Len & Gerry	Manhasset, New York

Gilbert, Ann	Los Angeles, California
Gilchrest, Frank	Newington, Connecticut
Gorremans, Rita & Jean	Antwerp, Belgium
Grella, Nancy & Mike	Brooklyn, New York
Hager, Brenda	Camarillo, California
Hand, Donna	Apalachin, New York
Hannan, Barbara	Lynbrook, New York
Healy, Tom	Downey, California
Heffernan, Tom	Dublin, Ireland
Heiman, Cay	Kansas City, Missouri
Henderson, Carl & Sheila	Addison, Illinois
Hess, George & Toni	St. Louis, Missouri
Hoffman, Phil & Joyce	Phoenix, Arizona
Holdren, Dick	Everett, Washington
Holly, Terry & Sheila	Pittsford, New York
Holt, Catherine	Snohomish, Washington
Hudson, Marion & Mark	Brooklyn, New York
Jelinek, Frank & Barbara	Westerville, Ohio
Kauer, Mike	Federal Way, Washington
Kearns, Tom	Merrick, New York
Kenny, Don & Chris	Redwood City, California
Kimball, Jim	Brooklyn, New York
Kruszewski, Dick	Queens, New York
Laing, Susie	Woodridge, Virginia
La Mar, Jeanne	Port Washington, New York
Le Jour, Jacques & Ging	Ghent, Belgium
Lucidi, Carl	Locust Valley, New York
Lyon, John	Massapequa, New York
Manfredi, Jimmy	Brooklyn, New York
Marchese, Joe	Rochester, New York
Martin, John & Louise	Garden City, New York
Matson, Wally	Danbury, Connecticut
McCafferty, Cindy & Bill	Columbus, Ohio
McCarthy, Bishop Edward	Phoenix, Arizona
McCarthy, Liz	Bethpage, New York

McDonnell, Kathleen	Dublin, Ireland
McDonnell, Mary	East Meadow, New York
McGilloway, Patrick	Staten Island, New York
McGuiness, Tom	Long Beach, California
McGuire, John & Donna	Tempe, Arizona
McSherry, Luke	Redding, Connecticut
Meehan, Rich	Palos Verdes, California
Menelly, Mario	Brooklyn, New York
Miles, Curt & Barbara	Columbia, Maryland
Moulton, Anne	Dublin, Ireland
Morgin, Lucille	San Jose, California
Morrow, Father Tom	Brooklyn, New York
Murphy, Dave & Eileen	Turnersville, New Jersey
Murphy, Father Jack	Seattle, Washington
Murphy, Mariann	Lindenhurst, New York
Murray, Father Ed	Bedford, Ohio
Nola, Mercedes	Toms River, New Jersey
O'Brien, Cathy	West Hempstead, New York
O'Donohoe, Seamus	Dublin, Ireland
Olsen, Oona	Bayville, New York
O'Rourke, Jim & Irene	Elmont, New York
O'Rourke, Father Tom	Queens, New York
O'Shea, Carbery	Seattle, Washington
Paglia, Chris & Don	New Haven, Connecticut
Pardi, Dick & Cindy	Woodland Hills, California
Pauly, Nancy	Beaverton, Oregon
Pfau, Father Bernie	Tolna, North Dakota
Purcell, Ginger	Oradell, New Jersey
Rasmussen, Jo	San Jose, California
Re, Ray & Beth	Glenside, Pennsylvania
Reber, Ethel & Bob	Sunnyvale, California
Regnier, Al	Los Angeles, California
Rigdon, Jan	Ballwin, Missouri
Rizzo, Joan	Brooklyn, New York
Roberts, Margie	Terryville, New York

Roney, Anne	Schenectady, New York
Rowell, Patty	Framingham, Massachusetts
Russak, Bonnie	Farmingdale, New York
Saabye, John	Bismarck, North Dakota
Samson, Margie	West Islip, New York
Sautner, Don	Queens, New York
Schaeffer, Fritz	Ballwin, Missouri
Schulteis, Sandy	Louisville, Kentucky
Sebetic, Joanne	Manhasset, New York
Sloun, Father Russ	Bronx, New York
Smith, Kevin & Carol	Boonton, New Jersey
Sobieski, Paul & Fran	Tempe, Arizona
Soenens, Bieke	Antwerp, Belgium
Stahl, Aileen & Vince	Milltown, New Jersey
Stanton, Bob	Slidell, Louisiana
Stemmle, Denis	Williamson, New York
Stritof, Sheri	Las Vegas, Nevada
Sullivan, George	Cincinnati, Ohio
Suntjens, Father Thieu	Belgium
Suriano, Chris	Pittsburgh, Pennsylvania
Tolfa, Jan	Monaca, Pennsylvania
Toner, Jim & Mary Pat	New Fairfield, Connecticut
Toner, Marian	Valley Cottage, New York
Toohil, John & Maryann	Syosset, New York
Toy, Tom	Massapequa Park, New York
Trujillo, Charlie & Rita	Tempe, Arizona
Turley, Bruce & Doris	Sayville, New York
Ulrich, Matt	Seattle, Washington
Van Dijck, Hugo	Louvain, Belgium
Van Reusel, Werner & Frits	Antwerp, Belgium
Vetter, Bernadette	Bismarck, North Dakota
Wallace, Wally & Dorothy	Staten Island, New York
Warner, Bob	Plainview, New York
Weiss, Fred & Kay	Lynbrook, New York

Wendt, John & Kay   Scottsdale, Arizona
Wolfe, Father George   Reno, Nevada
Yudt. Hank & Judy   Syosset, New York
Zech, Jomy & Betty-June   Seattle, Washington